HOMESCHOOL NOW

Getting Started and Insider Tips for K-12

Beth Spann

ISBN: 9798361677610

Cover design by: pixelstudio
Printed in the United States of America

CONTENTS

INTRODUCTION

At the age of twenty-six, I had never heard of homeschooling. Recently having graduated from optometry school, I began working full-time as an eye doctor in Tennessee. I was unmarried and ready to enjoy life without the burden of school. Having children of my own one day was a fleeting thought.

During my first year of working, I began seeing families who homeschooled their children. At first, I didn't give it much thought other than it seemed a little "out there," but over time, one thing became increasingly clear. These homeschooled kids were pleasant, interesting, and could quickly maneuver through an eye exam. I looked forward to seeing them.

From my first interaction with a homeschooling family, it would be another two years before I was married, four years before I would have the first of my two children, and ten years before my first child would start kindergarten. While I didn't realize it then, our homeschool had been years in the making and began during those early years of practicing optometry. It eventually led our family down a path I previously hadn't known existed.

Growing up, I was a student in the West Virginia public school system. I have great memories from elementary through high school. My graduating senior class had just under three hundred students. Many of us had gone to school together since kindergarten. Because our high school was small compared to most high schools today, the teachers and administrators knew the students and, in many cases, the families quite well. This familiarity fostered a closeness in the school that helped with discipline and academic problems. However, the school didn't offer much outside mainstream classes due to its size. The basics were covered, but that was about all.

I declared during my senior year that I wanted to major in accounting in college. Was it because I had taken an accounting class in high school? No. My school didn't offer such a class. Was it because I had spent time with an accountant and thought this would be a great career choice? No. I probably didn't give it that much thought. I chose accounting because it sounded good. And to throw a little icing on the cake, I added pre-law to make it sound even better. Yes, I had decided with absolutely no knowledge that I would be an accountant and then go on to law school. The August after I graduated from high school, I began my college education at a university twenty-four hours away from home. I had no significant scholarship money and no idea who I was or what I truly wanted to be.

You may say that's what college is for - to find yourself. But, after paying back significant student loans for years, I would say that is bad advice. So many people make life-altering decisions in their teens and early twenties that sometimes saddle them for decades. Unfortunately, I was one of those people.

Two universities and three college majors later, I decided without ever having an eye exam that I wanted to be an optometrist, and I applied to optometry school. After completing four additional years of schooling, I graduated from optometry school with a Bachelor of Science degree and a Doctorate of Optometry degree. These two degrees also came with six-figure debt and a career that had been chosen somewhat randomly.

I worked as an optometrist for six years before having my first child. Fast forward several years, and I now had a daughter ready to start kindergarten. I attended an informational session at the private school we had chosen for her and left the meeting completely panicked. I didn't like it! My gut feeling said this wasn't the place for us. But unfortunately, we had no Plan B.

I went home and called my mom. When I paused to take a breath, she said the crazy word "homeschool."

"What, Mom?" Surely, she didn't just say that.

"You've commented several times over the past few years how well-behaved and smart your homeschooled patients are. Why don't you homeschool Katherine for kindergarten?"

"What, Mom?"

"You heard me. Try homeschooling, and if it doesn't work, put her in school somewhere for first grade. I've always thought it would have been nice to have homeschooled you and your sister."

"WHAT, MOM?!!"

I took her advice. My daughter started kindergarten that year as a homeschooler. Her younger brother joined in, and we never looked back.

In the early years, I wanted to give my children a good start academically and instill in them a love of learning. Then, as they got older, I tailored their education to help them find their strengths and interests. I didn't want them to approach their future with the same randomness and uncertainty I had once had. Fourteen years later, I can honestly say that homeschooling has been one of the best decisions I've ever made. Without a doubt, our entire family has been truly blessed through this experience.

This book answers the ten most common questions I've been asked about homeschooling over the years. These are also the same questions that I had when I began homeschooling. The following pages are an account of our journey with specific details of how we homeschooled, including a daily schedule sample, examples of yearly plans, and a list of some of our favorite curriculums. It chronicles our successes and failures along the way and my personal thoughts and tips for elementary, middle, and high school.

We currently live in a social climate that is deeply divided. What is written in this book is based on my experience and opinions. That said, I have absolutely no problem "agreeing to disagree." I think that's one of the attributes of homeschooling that makes it great. You are the parent who has taken on the responsibility of homeschooling your child or children. This means you get to make the decisions. Your kids aren't my kids. They all have different strengths and personalities. What works for one child may not work for the next one, even a sibling. And that's okay. Everyone's homeschooling looks different. This book is just one example that gives you a glimpse into our world. Glean from it what you want or reject all of it. If you are thinking about homeschooling, the decisions are yours, and that's a great place to be. I hope you can learn from our mistakes and successes and realize you don't have to be perfect to educate your children at home.

WHY HOMESCHOOL?

The year my daughter started kindergarten, we were by no means surrounded by a multitude of homeschoolers. It wasn't until the school systems introduced Common Core that we started seeing a sudden growth in our homeschooling community. The numbers continued to increase steadily over the years until the COVID-19 pandemic sent students home from school. Since then, homeschooling has exploded across the country. Parents that have always said "never," "not me," or "yeah, right" are considering it and asking for advice on how it works and where to start.

At this point, let me stop and say that I do not think homeschooling is for everyone. But I do think if it even crosses your mind as a possibility, it's worth exploring.

Fourteen years ago, these were the reasons I started homeschooling:

- My daughter already knew how to read and count, and I was afraid she wouldn't learn anything new in kindergarten.
- One of my distinct childhood memories is how chaotic, stressful, and rushed our school mornings were. I didn't want that for my kids.
- I wanted to give my daughter a good start in math.

- I was working part-time to make my student loan payments and would have had to work full-time and put my younger son in daycare to afford the private school we were considering. (Our public school was also an option, but after doing my research, I felt homeschooling would be a better fit.)
- And finally, the most important reason I decided to homeschool was that I wanted to protect my kids' childhoods. I didn't want them to learn things at school that I felt they were too young to know. I also wanted them to have free time to play and be kids without having to do hours of homework at night. I believe in letting kids be kids, and I knew it could be that way if we homeschooled.

These were my reasons when I first started. Those reasons began to change as we homeschooled through middle and high school. I wanted to help my daughter and son to know themselves. I wanted them to find out what their strengths are and where their interests lie. What do they find fascinating? What do they find boring? As we exposed them to different things I'll explore in later chapters, we started seeing a clear path in their interests and natural talents and focused more heavily on those things.

Parents choose to educate their children at home for many reasons. Below are some of the more common ones I've heard from others over the years.

- Religious reasons
- Child is unvaccinated.
- Parent has safety concerns for their child.
- Child is being bullied.
- Parent is unhappy with the curriculum taught in schools.
- Child resides in an underperforming school district.
- Parent wants to be the primary influence on the child.
- Parent is concerned about their child's friends at school.

- Child is academically advanced.
- Child is struggling socially in school.
- Child is struggling academically in school.

WHAT DOES IT TAKE TO HOMESCHOOL?

Many things help to make a good homeschool. Love and patience certainly come to mind, but those are a given. Well-behaved kids would be a definite bonus. But as I tried to pare it down to the bare bones of what it takes to homeschool effectively - selflessness, curriculum, and confidence are three absolute necessities.

Selflessness

Let me stress the importance of selflessness. Foremost, you need to rethink homeschooling if you're not willing to give up social media, Netflix, tennis, or whatever your hobbies are during school hours. I had a Facebook friend who homeschooled her four kids. She continuously posted and replied daily about how their homeschooling wasn't going well - along with selfies, memes, and pictures of her food. To be successful in homeschooling, you need to give your full attention to your children during the school day, especially the younger ones. These are the years to start building a solid foundation for their education. You want them to love to learn, which becomes difficult if they're always waiting for their mom or dad to get their face out of their phone. Instagram is not more important than your children or their education, and they should never be made to feel that it is.

Distractions and disruptions are unavoidable. Life happens. But your kids shouldn't have to school around your personal sc on a regular basis. They deserve the same or better instruction as what they would get at a public school. You've taken on their education. Do it well.

If you need more personal time during the day, choose your children's curriculum with that in mind. They will likely have independent work time when you can do some things for yourself. But remember, what you choose needs to work for you and them. For example, if they aren't learning to spell with the workbooks you've chosen, you'll need to consider a different curriculum that may require more time and effort on your part.

Curriculum

On a materials level, it takes curriculum. It doesn't have to be the most expensive or newest curriculum; it can be purchased, borrowed, or free. The most important thing is that it's the right one for you and your child. I recommend researching online, asking other parents their opinions, and possibly attending a curriculum fair to evaluate homeschooling materials in person. I've always chosen what we use by asking: 1) Is this something I can teach, and 2) will this help my children learn?

For example, several people recommended Math-U-See for our math curriculum when we first started homeschooling. I went to a homeschool fair, thought it looked great and decided to watch a sample video lesson at home. Despite my best efforts, I couldn't stay awake while watching it. The video was well-made, and Math-U-See is an excellent curriculum, especially for parents who don't enjoy math. But the gentleman's voice lulled me to sleep every time I tried to watch the lesson. It just wasn't going to work. I then looked at Saxon Math, another highly recommended and solid math curriculum. I browsed through the first several lessons in a first-grade book and realized my daughter had already learned most of the material. After further investigation, it didn't seem like the right fit for us. I later came across Singapore Math and immediately knew this one would work. The illustrations were colorful and interesting, and I liked the approach used to teach math. It turned out to be a challenging curriculum, and by the time my daughter reached fifth grade, I was spending a lot of time relearning the subject and seeking out people to help me solve word problems. Looking back, however, it was well worth it. It turned out to be a fantastic curriculum for both of my kids and, with a little extra effort, was something that I could teach. Note that a good curriculum isn't necessarily an easy one. Learning and teaching can be hard work.

Choosing a curriculum is something you need to spend quality time on. I cannot stress this enough. I've seen parents switch curriculums four times in one year. Doing that can cause gaps in your child's education, leading to frustration for everyone down the road. Instead, make well-informed choices and stick with them, especially for the core subjects, like grammar and math, that build on concepts from chapter to chapter and year to year. Only change the curriculum if you've given it a fair chance and it's not working. Remember that continuity is essential to building a solid foundation in several subjects. Also, remember that the most expensive curriculums aren't always the best. We've paid a lot for some, and for others, we've borrowed or gotten online for free. When my kids were still in elementary school, I even created my own curriculum for a few of their classes using online resources and books from the library.

Confidence

I debated whether to add this to the list, but I do think confidence is necessary to homeschool. You want your kids to feel like they won the lottery by being homeschooled, and in my opinion, they did! If you express doubts or insecurities about doing it, that may affect how they perceive themselves and their situation.

Another important reason for confidence is that it's hard to avoid the naysayers. After fourteen years of homeschooling, I still have people telling me I shouldn't homeschool my kids for various reasons they feel are valid. For example, last year, a teacher told me she felt sorry for my kids because they missed high school football games. I resisted the urge to go on and on about how my children have benefitted from homeschooling in so many other ways. So instead, I have a standard response. I'll say, "Oh! I certainly don't think homeschooling's for everyone, but it works well for us." I'll then smile and change the subject or walk away.

There are some people you will never convince that homeschooling is a good option, so don't waste your time. Instead, spend that energy on your kids. Use my response or come up with your own, but don't let others, especially strangers or acquaintances, tell you what is best for your child.

Family, however, can be a little harder to navigate. Most extended families have varying opinions on homeschooling, and many feel they have a stake in how you raise your children. The best way to show them that you've made the right choice is to homeschool well. Be prepared daily, get organized, and go "all in" on homeschooling. If you're giving it your best, then your best is enough. If you have doubts or lack confidence, some of that will melt away as you see your child excel under your watch. Decide what you want to share and not share with extended family. It's your homeschool. Your child. Your decision.

Also, know that you don't have to be a professional teacher to be successful. Sometimes teachers have the most challenging time homeschooling their own children because they've been trained a certain way and have trouble breaking away from that. For example, a teacher I met pulled her child out of school due to bullying. This mother set up her homeschool like a public school, including bells to end class and a specific time for everything, including lunch and recess. The child also had to sit at his desk the whole day. This mother was very loving but couldn't enjoy the flexibility of homeschooling due to her training. Her child asked to go back to public school the following year.

Ultimately, I think the best way to be confident is to be prepared. Do your research. Decide what your children will study each year and what curriculum you'll use. Talk to other parents who homeschool. Find out what's available in your area for homeschoolers. Don't forget to add some fun! My kids used to get asked all the time if they liked being homeschooled. When your bright, happy child says they love it, it's a real confidence booster.

Lastly, even seasoned homeschool parents sometimes have doubts. When my kids were in elementary school, I was in a homeschool support group for moms. There were some there who had homeschooled for a decade or longer. I gleaned everything I could from them each month when we met. One night, a mother of four kids brought her daily planner to the meeting. Believe it or not, most of us had never seen someone else's schedule. Every mom in the room savored looking at it. We were curious how she balanced three kids and a baby each day. What subjects did she teach the kids together? How many school subjects did she do in a day? How much time did she allow for each subject? Even though most of us in the room had homeschooled for more than a few years, we loved that she was willing to be vulnerable and share this with us. That night gave most of us some fresh ideas and reinforced what we were doing at home. Being around other homeschooling parents and asking questions has been a game-changer for us and has helped give me the confidence to homeschool through high school.

WHERE DO I START?

A close friend of mine pulled her children out of public school last year and asked what she needed to do to start homeschooling. Several homeschoolers at our church gave her advice on how to get started, where she could register her kids, curriculum choices, and how to find extracurricular academic and sports teams. She was asked by other parents, who also wanted to start homeschooling, how she knew what to do and how she did it so quickly. She told me that most of the parents she meets who want to pull their kids out of public schools have no idea where to start.

There are seven steps listed below to guide you through this process. Homeschooling varies greatly based on where you live and your personal choices, so I've also recommended a few websites as good starting points to research some of these steps.

➤ Step 1 – Look up your state's rules and regulations and register your child, if required.

All states have different rules and regulations for homeschooling that you must read to ensure eligibility and compliance. The first place to look is the Homeschool Legal Defense Association's website, HSLDA.org. This non-profit homeschool advocacy organization helps protect your right to homeschool and provides educational support. Their website is easy to navigate, gives detailed information on how to withdraw from public school, and lists the homeschool laws for every state, including testing requirements and mandatory subjects. The HSLDA website also shows a map that places each state into one of four categories based on how strict or lenient the rules are for homeschooling. Note that within these categories, state laws still vary.

Category 1
No Notice (is required to be given to the state of your intent to homeschool), Low Regulation
Category 2
Low Regulation
Category 3
Moderate Regulation
Category 4
High Regulation

For example, Texas is a "No Notice, Low Regulation" state. Homeschools are considered private schools, and you are required to:

1. Use a written or online curriculum to teach math, reading, and spelling/grammar.
2. Teach a course in good citizenship.

Tennessee is a "Low Regulation" state. Here you are required to:

1. Teach your child for a minimum of 180 days each school year.
2. Register through your local school district, a church-related school, or a category three distance-learning school. HSLDA.org gives you the information required for each option to make the best decision for your family.

We live in a low regulation state and register through a church-related school. We pay a registration fee, and they provide a counselor, yearly testing, a homeschool teacher ID card, and maintain our student records. This school also awards a high school diploma, sends official transcripts to colleges and universities, and provides a high school graduation ceremony.

New York is a "High Regulation" state. Here you are required to:

1. Submit a notice of intent to homeschool to the school district superintendent.
2. Submit an IHIP (Individualized Home Instruction Plan), including syllabi, curriculum, textbooks, instruction plans, and who will teach your child.
3. Report homeschooled days and hours to meet state requirements.
4. File quarterly reports.
5. Submit an annual assessment of each homeschooled child either by standardized testing or a written narrative evaluation by an approved evaluator.

Each state has different rules and regulations, and I would highly recommend that you familiarize yourself with what your state requires. However, don't let the lack of regulation or over-regulation of a particular state scare you away from homeschooling. It may seem overwhelming initially but take it one step at a time. It will become easier as you gain more experience. Also, reach out to more experienced homeschoolers. They can give you great information and sometimes save you a lot of time.

➤ Step 2 - Determine what subjects you need to teach and research curriculums.

The amount of curriculum choices available to homeschoolers is overwhelming. In the following chapters, I'll talk more about this. I have always used cathyduffyreviews.com to help narrow down the choices. Her website is a wealth of information, and I highly recommend starting your online search there. Most states' rules and regulations will directly or indirectly determine what subjects you teach. If not, as you research curriculums, it should become apparent what is typically taught in each grade.

➤ Step 3 – Decide if you value a particular educational approach or philosophy.

Several approaches, or philosophies, exist to educate your child outside the traditional textbook approach used in public schools. In the next chapter, I'll discuss the more common ones. These different approaches to learning can allow for homeschooling to be a highly tailored education for your child.

➤ Step 4 – Explore options to homeschool outside the home.

While we've done most of our homeschooling at home, I have outsourced some classes and activities along the way for various reasons. One reason was that I wanted my daughter and son to spend time with kids their ages and make friends. It's great that homeschooled children have a reputation for easily speaking with adults, but they also need to know how to connect with their peers.

I also realized having someone else teach certain subjects might be more effective. For example, it was hard for me to be objective when grading writing assignments as my kids got older, so putting them in a writing class was a better way for them to learn and receive good feedback.

And finally, when you're with your children around the clock, you need some time to run errands and schedule appointments. Having your kids involved in classes or activities outside the home is a great time to do that.

In Chapter 5, I'll discuss the pros and cons of the different opportunities available to us over the past fourteen years – most of which are offered in homeschooling communities across the country now.

➤ Step 5 – Plan your year.

Some states require a yearly plan, but if yours doesn't, I would still recommend you do one. A yearly plan benefits you by having your goals written down for each child for the upcoming year. It's not a detailed schedule but more of a guideline that keeps you on track and documents what curriculum you want to use for each subject and what you hope to accomplish for the year. Once the school year gets into full swing and life gets busy, having something to refer to can keep your homeschooling on track.

Having a general plan has also helped me recognize valuable field trips and learning opportunities over the years that have complemented our curriculum or made the learning more fun.

Of course, we all realize plans may need to change. Sometimes goals need to be re-evaluated, and that's okay. A yearly plan simply helps get you organized before the school year begins.

After trying several store-bought and online planners the first few years, I finally made my own with Excel, printed it, and took it to FedEx for spiral binding (all for about seven dollars). In the back of the planner, I included our yearly plan for each subject for each child. It was basic and straightforward, but that's all I needed. Planning is important, especially if you're not using a curriculum that does it for you.

Appendix A shows two examples of our yearly plans. Our long-term goals always helped us to stay or get back on track to finish the school year on time.

➤ Step 6 – Make space for homeschooling.

During the first two years we homeschooled, we used the kitchen table, and I turned a coat closet into my office, where I kept our books and materials together in one place. I eventually turned our playroom into a homeschool room and bought two desks and some bookshelves. I wasn't a stickler about where my kids did their schoolwork if they tried their best and completed the assignments. My son's favorite place was lying on the floor, and my daughter preferred to be next to a window. Despite my kids not sitting upright at a desk day after day (which surprisingly bothers more people than you would think), my kids have done fine. My daughter recently completed her first year away at college and did very well. Ironically, several of her college classes were available by streaming, and she didn't even get out of bed to attend class.

Even our homeschooling standards were a bit higher than that! The bottom line is that your homeschooled kids need a place to do their work comfortably with the least amount of distraction.

➤ Step 7 – Begin homeschooling your child.

You're ready! When you first start homeschooling, don't be too hard on yourself. Even with the best planning, you'll likely need to adjust. The most important thing is not to give up. Keep trying to improve things that aren't working. Rearrange the schedule. Take more breaks. Take fewer breaks. Add in a fun morning snack as a treat for finishing schoolwork. Do what you need to do to make your homeschooling successful. I once offered my kids ten bucks each if they went upstairs and learned their multiplication tables. If they could still remember them one week later, they both got another ten bucks. That was the best forty dollars I've ever spent. They needed extra motivation for that massive assignment, and I needed a break. Keep working to find what works best for you and your children.

WHAT ARE EDUCATIONAL PHILOSOPHIES?

A s mentioned previously, there are different philosophies, or approaches, to educating children. The five most common homeschooling methods are traditional, classical, Charlotte Mason, unit studies, and eclectic (or mixed). There are a few others, such as Montessori and Waldorf, but they are less common in homeschooling and will not be discussed here. Below is a brief description of each philosophy to give you a basic overview. I would suggest doing more research online. Again, HSLDA.org is an excellent place to start. And, remember, one method of homeschooling isn't necessarily better than another. Ultimately, it comes down to what works best for your family.

Traditional (School-at-Home)
This method is likely how you were educated if you went to public school. You have traditional textbooks and workbooks. Your child reads an assigned chapter, completes a related workbook page or questions, and is given tests to determine retention of the material. Textbooks are usually chosen independently for each subject.

Homeschooling this way is a nice option if you think it might be temporary or plan to put your child back in a public or private school. A traditional approach could make that transition easier. However, it can also be a lot of work for the teaching parent, especially if multiple children are homeschooled in different grades. A traditional approach worked best for us for math and grammar.

Classical

The classical method is a very popular and well-proven way to educate children, with its origins dating back thousands of years. This approach divides learning into three stages called the trivium. The first, the grammar stage, focuses on teaching elementary-aged children extensive facts to memorize in the different subjects. The second, the dialectic stage, teaches students in the middle grades how to think. And lastly, the rhetoric stage instructs high school students on how to express their thoughts.

This method is rigorous and systematic. The school subjects are taught around a central historical timeline. For example, suppose your child is learning about the Renaissance. In that case, they might also read Chaucer or Shakespeare and study earth science and basic astronomy - all notable during this period of history. It focuses on reading the great books (ancient and modern), studying Latin or classical Greek, learning logic, and eventually expressing thoughts in an organized, informed manner.

When we first started homeschooling, I followed the recommendations in the book *The Well-Trained Mind: A Guide to Classical Education at Home* by Susan Wise Bauer and Jesse Wise. The authors of this book favor a classical approach to homeschooling. A year later, we joined a Classical Conversations community that met one day a week and taught classes using this method. I'm glad we tried it, and during this time, my kids could recite facts well above their grade level, but this type of learning style just wasn't for us.

Several of my close friends love this approach, and their kids excel. However, I felt we needed to commit all twelve years to a classical curriculum to benefit fully. What was the point of my young kids spending hours every week memorizing facts (that they didn't understand) and forming the basic building blocks for the next stage unless we moved on to that next stage? I'll say it again. This is a very systematic approach to educating, and each stage of the trivium relies on the others being executed properly.

Teaching history was the one aspect of the classical approach I absolutely loved. It was fascinating to learn what was happening in other parts of the world, especially during biblical times. Learning it in chronological order, rather than in snippets here and there, made it come to life. I continued to teach history with this approach throughout elementary and middle school. We also incorporated reading assignments, art, and geography activities into our studies that correlated with the period we were studying. This was something my kids could do together and I adjusted the assignments accordingly. I chose independent science and math curriculums, and we picked Spanish over Latin. I know that many feel if you know Latin, other languages will be easier to learn. But my thinking was that we probably wouldn't have the time to learn multiple languages. Spanish and American Sign Language are the two languages I have needed as an adult, so we moved on from Latin quickly.

If you search for "classical homeschool curriculum," you'll find plenty to choose from and instructions on how to teach using this philosophy.

Resources:
WellTrainedMind.com
Classicalcurriculum.com
VeritasPress.com

Charlotte Mason

Charlotte Mason, a British educator in the late 1800s and early 1900s, firmly believed that not just the mind but the whole person must be educated. She said, "Education is an Atmosphere, a Discipline, a Life." She believed that your child's education should come from values at home, from developing good habits and character, from academics using "living books" rather than textbooks, and by forming ideas as opposed to just learning facts.

"Living books" are books written in narrative form by an author with a passion for the subject. Students must narrate what they've read to digest the material rather than take multiple choice or fill-in-the-blank tests. Because each child conveys to you the material they have learned, several subjects like history, literature, and geography can be taught to multiple children at once. In contrast, a subject like math would likely be taught individually. The Charlotte Mason approach utilizes short lessons and encourages nature walks, observation, journaling, and history portfolios as part of the learning process.

While we have never fully committed to this approach, it's attractive to many families. I tried it with my daughter in early elementary with handwriting. While we had a separate handwriting workbook, I also chose rich, well-constructed sentences for her to copy on paper from the Little House series of books we were reading. Doing this helped with her handwriting skills and exposed her to larger spelling words and expert sentence construction.

I can see strong value in the Charlotte Mason approach to homeschooling, but overall, it wasn't the best fit for us. I was concerned there would be gaps in my kids' education that I may not catch. Nevertheless, it's a philosophy worth researching and learning more about how to do it well. You may fully embrace it or add components of it into your homeschool studies as we did. An internet search using "Charlotte Mason homeschool" will direct you to more information about this educational philosophy.

Resources:
AmblesideOnline.org
SimplyCharlotteMason.com

Unit Studies

Unit studies incorporate teaching many school subjects into a theme or topic. A simple example would be a unit study on ancient Egypt. Your child would:

- Read books on Egypt (history)
- Build a pyramid with sugar cubes (art)
- Make a salt map of the country (geography/art)
- Learn the shape of a pyramid (math)
- Read a fictional book set in ancient Egypt (literature)
- Learn how the Egyptians used the Nile River to irrigate their farmland (science/geography)
- Learn how to spell words such as pyramid, sphinx, and pharaoh (spelling)
- Take a field trip to a museum that displays ancient Egyptian artifacts

Unit studies can be a stand-alone homeschooling method, or they can be easily integrated into any of the other educational philosophies. For example, you can use a Charlotte Mason approach by using only "living books" in your unit study. One that embraces a classical philosophy might use a chronological approach to history as its central theme to cover many subjects.

Some benefits of using unit studies are that they can be a fun way to learn, and you can teach multiple grades at one time by adjusting the assignments for each child. In addition, you can purchase a complete curriculum based on unit studies or simply do a unit study for a topic you want to explore more. I chose to do a few unit studies when my kids were in elementary school that I put together myself. One was on safety, and we learned about stranger danger, bicycle safety, and fire safety. I used materials from our local police department and online resources to teach it. The kids helped me put together a fire escape plan for our house, and we incorporated a few field trips, like bike rides and a visit to a fire station.

I never taught unit studies as our primary curriculum for a few reasons. First, they tend to require significant preparation before teaching, even the purchased ones. Second, I was concerned there would be gaps in my kids' education in some subjects. However, these are so fun to do with young children that I would recommend purchasing one or making your own and giving it a try, even if it's not how you plan to teach regularly. If you choose to do one, but not as a complete curriculum, make it about something that interests your children: cars, baking, a particular holiday, sports, etc. A quick online search will give you great ideas, many of which are free. It's activities like these that make great homeschooling memories for everyone.

Resources:
TheHomeschoolMom.com (Search unit studies and reviews)

Eclectic or Mixed

Our family has used all the previous approaches to homeschooling over the past fourteen years. This method is called eclectic homeschooling, and most families we know homeschool this way. For us, it's been the best of all worlds. We've chosen rich, well-written math, language arts, and science textbooks. Still, we've taken advantage of all the different homeschooling approaches outside traditional learning for history, art, music, social studies, and other subjects. It's allowed my children to have a solid education in the core subjects while having fun and developing a love of learning in less traditional ways. It's all about finding what works best for you and your children. You need to be aware of what's available to help you make those decisions. This takes a little research and reaching out to others about what has worked for them.

A Note About Unschooling

Unschooling is sometimes called self-directed homeschooling or delight-directed homeschooling. There is no curriculum or testing involved with this approach. For example, if your child is interested in horses, you provide information on horses until the child is ready to learn about something else. Your children need to be motivated to learn on their own.

While providing information and experiences for your child about things they're interested in is good parenting, homeschooling requires more than this. It is my opinion that this is a risky way to take control of your child's learning. You have taken on the responsibility of teaching them; they deserve a solid and complete education.

I've heard parents say they're "teaching good character," which is terrific. Hopefully, we all are, but children still need basic life skills and knowledge. What if you can't continue homeschooling and you need to enroll your child in public school? What if you have a child that develops an interest in engineering in high school but doesn't have the basic math skills to pursue their dream? What if your child wants to attend college but can't read well enough to pass an admissions test? What if your child wants to pursue a career that requires a high school diploma and not a GED? In most states, you must complete a required amount of coursework to qualify for a high school diploma.

Don't hold your child back because you don't know where to start with homeschooling, are too busy with work or other kids, can't afford the curriculum, or think this is the best approach. Do your research. There is an abundance of help available. It would be a shame to short-change your child on their education.

HOW DO I FIND THE RIGHT CURRICULUM?

To find a dedicated curriculum for each of the five philosophies discussed in the previous chapter, I highly recommend cathyduffyreviews.com to start your search. On this site, when you click on a curriculum choice, the right side of the page will display an "Instant Key" that will tell you which educational approach is used. You may notice that many of the curriculums have multiple approaches listed. This is due to overlap between philosophies and is based on how you implement the material. The summary on the same page will explain the different aspects of the curriculum that allow it to be listed in more than one category.

When you begin researching, you may notice that there is not only a multitude of curriculums available for each educational philosophy, but these learning materials come in various formats. These formats are discussed below.

All-in-One or Box Curriculum Package
- Everything you need to homeschool a particular grade is sent to you in one box (or boxes), complete with plans for the entire

academic year. Some of these curriculums will utilize a hybrid approach by also including online materials.

- Depending on which all-in-one curriculum you choose, the learning materials will be presented using a traditional, classical, Charlotte Mason, unit study, or an eclectic teaching philosophy.
- Box curriculums can include teacher's guides, books, workbooks, and tests. Some companies will even help with record keeping and grading. Many give you options and let you build your curriculum with the different products they offer.
- Box curriculums are a convenient and great option if you want your teaching planned by professionals and want reassurance that you have all bases covered.
- Most of what is included in these all-in-one curriculums can also be purchased separately, so if you love the history lessons but not the language arts, you can pick and choose.
- Be careful when ordering an entire grade-level curriculum. Depending on your child's strength in each subject, you may end up with products you can't use due to being too easy or too hard. Some of the curriculum packages offer placement tests.
- The all-in-one packages tend to be a bit pricey upfront and can be a lot of work for the child and parent.

Online Curriculum

- Online curriculums are numerous and can range from full-curriculum packages to a single class. Different options are available utilizing traditional, classical, Charlotte Mason, unit studies, and eclectic educational philosophies.
- Depending on which one(s) you choose - teaching, assignments, and grading may all be done for the parent.
- The price can range from free to thousands of dollars per year. There are so many of these programs available now that it would be wise to research thoroughly and look at reviews to determine which ones are worthy of your time and

money. Not all are created equally. I recommend choosing the homeschool philosophy that interests you and searching for online curriculums that align with that.

- If you plan to use a complete (full curriculum) online program, I recommend finding one that will perform placement tests to determine where your child is academically. Doing this can save time, money, and frustration.
- This option may not allow the flexibility in schedule that many homeschoolers enjoy.

Unit Studies

- As discussed previously, unit studies can stand alone or be designed to follow a traditional, Charlotte Mason, classical, or eclectic approach, depending on the materials used and how they're implemented.
- Unit studies vary widely in price depending on what you choose to buy. Or they can be free if you do it yourself. There are many free unit study plans available online.
- Unit studies can be considerable work for the parent to prepare and teach, but it's worth it if your kids learn and have fun at the same time!

Á La Carte

- You can still stay true to an educational philosophy by selecting teaching material á la carte for each subject rather than purchasing an all-in-one, online, or unit study curriculum.
  - To teach using a traditional approach, you will choose a textbook or workbook for each subject, like what your child might use in a public school.
  - To stay true to the Charlotte Mason approach, you will use "living books."
  - To embrace a classical approach, you will use books and great literature and follow a chronological approach to

learning.

- ◦ To use an eclectic approach to homeschooling, you will choose a curriculum for each subject based on what you think will work well for your children, regardless of which educational method is used.
- Choosing a curriculum for individual subjects gives you, the parent, the flexibility to select from all that's available for your preferred educational philosophy. It allows you to choose the richest and most effective learning materials tailored to your child's needs.
- This approach to selecting a curriculum requires research from the teaching parent.
- This method can be budget-friendly. It's the way I bought most of our curriculum. I used inexpensive, borrowed, or free materials for some subjects, which allowed me to spend more on other curriculums that I wanted to use.

An online search of each philosophy will lead you to many curriculum choices available. Christianbook.com and Rainbowresourse.com are great online stores that allow you to search curriculums for each educational approach.

WHAT IS AVAILABLE OUTSIDE THE HOME?

O nce we became involved in the local homeschooling community, the options for activities and classes outside our home seemed limitless, even overwhelming at times. Below are some of the opportunities available to us over the years. Many of these have been invaluable. They've enhanced my children's education and helped them become more well-rounded individuals.

Sometimes it can be challenging to find this information. Local homeschool Facebook groups and other online forums are excellent places to start. Talking to other homeschooling parents in your area, especially those with older kids, can be a wealth of information. Not only can you gather information, but you can get opinions and advice as well. And lastly, most states have a home educator association that can lead you to local chapters. These organizations usually have information on what is offered in your area. An internet search should lead you to these for each state.

Co-ops
A popular option for many homeschooling families is co-ops.

These communities come together and parents teach or hire instructors for various courses. They typically meet one day a week so the students can be home the remaining days to do assigned material from their classes and other coursework taught at home.

Co-ops can vary greatly. One that we joined had five hundred students, a co-op principal, and paid teachers. My kids took theater, ballroom dance, chess, art, and writing classes there. This co-op offered courses for kindergarten through twelfth grade that ranged from ukulele lessons to geometry to art history. Parents could pick and choose what classes they wanted their children to take. I was able to drop my kids off and was required to be a parent volunteer sixteen hours per semester. We paid each teacher monthly.

A few years later, we joined a smaller co-op for middle and high school students only. This one also had classes taught by paid teachers, many of them professionals in the subject they were teaching. We paid for the classes up front for the whole school year, and I was, again, required to do volunteer hours.

I have a few friends that have started their own co-ops with like-minded families – whether it's common homeschool philosophies, religious beliefs, secular beliefs, or just friends who want to homeschool their kids together. Often these are free because the participating parents take on the teaching responsibilities.

While the co-ops we joined used a more traditional, if not eclectic approach to teaching, co-ops that wholly embrace the Charlotte Mason, classical, and unit study learning philosophies are also available.

Lastly, we now have a few private, faith-based schools in our area that offer a hybrid approach to schooling, also called a university model. Students attend school three days a week and are home the other two days to complete assignments. While this is technically not homeschooling but private school, many parents feel this is the best of both worlds. It's an excellent option for families who can't or don't want to take on the responsibility of their child's education or choose their curriculum. As a result, parents have less input on the learning process but still have some of the great flexibility homeschooling offers.

Parent Support Groups

I have been part of two very different parent support groups over the years. A fellow homeschool mom started the first one that I previously mentioned. About a dozen women met at her house monthly, where she would have a guest speaker or a specific topic to discuss. I didn't have much in common with these women. In fact, I didn't agree with them on many things, including homeschooling philosophies. However, those five years I met with them absolutely helped shape our homeschool. I gleaned an amazing amount of information from these women. If you're willing to listen, you can still learn from people with different goals and objectives than you.

I also joined a second, larger support group through a local church during that time. It offered student competitions and field trips and had over a hundred members. By this time, my kids were approaching middle school, and this group allowed them to participate in competitions like MATHCOUNTS, Science Bowl, Science Olympiad, spelling and geography bees, and a Scholar's Bowl team.

We are still part of this second group. The church provides the place to meet, but it's the parents who register the teams and coach the kids. My son's middle school Science Bowl team won the opportunity to represent our state in Washington, D.C. Another group went to two National Science Olympiad competitions to compete against top science students from all over the country.

There are many opportunities and successful students educated at home who are doing amazing things. None of this happens by accident, though. They work hard and have adults willing to invest time in them. Parent support groups can be whatever meets the needs of those involved. If you can't find what you're looking for, you can always start a group yourself.

Competition teams

Parent support groups aren't the only places to find competition teams. For several years, my kids competed in Science Olympiad at the local level against a homeschool team from a small private co-op. My daughter also joined a CyberPatriot team in high school that was independently started by a mother whose son was interested in competing. This mother asked the director of cybersecurity of a large company to be the coach, and he said yes.

There are many opportunities like this available to homeschoolers; obviously, not all are science related. If there is a team or competition that your child wants to do, find out if it's available in your community. If not, start your own as this mother did. She didn't know the first thing about cybersecurity, but she made it work.

Field Trip Groups

We participated in field trip groups to meet other homeschoolers and to get group discounts. I usually found out about these groups on social media. It was always fun, but once we made good homeschooling friends, we planned our own field trips to explore caves, tour an ice cream plant, visit museums, and even visit an optician to make a pair of glasses. We went to many places and had some unique experiences that wouldn't have been possible with a busload of kids. We found that most businesses love homeschool groups. Usually, their parents are present, the students are well-behaved, and they ask good questions. These field trips are some of my sweetest memories of our early years of homeschooling. We had so much fun! Unfortunately, as my kids got older, there was simply less time to do activities like this. So don't forget to plan some fun outings for your young ones!

Public and Private School Classes

In some public and private schools, homeschoolers are welcome to take classes with the enrolled students for a fee. Doing this might benefit a homeschooled student who wants to take an advanced or AP class not offered elsewhere or if the course is less expensive through the local school than it would be through a co-op, online program, or local community college. If interested, this option varies widely, so it would be best to call directly to check a school's policy.

Private Businesses

Many private businesses also like to cater to homeschoolers. They know these parents are spending money on their children, and the students are available during the weekdays while other kids are at school. My kids attended a weekly class at a local science museum one year. Our group had enough kids that the museum created this class, especially for them. As I'll mention in a later chapter, our local YMCA started a homeschool PE class that was four hours every week and only cost twenty dollars per child each month. Also, we live near a tourist area with several attractions and museums that offer "homeschool days" with deep discounts on admission. However, many businesses will provide daily deals on products and entertainment if you can show them a homeschool teacher ID card.

Sports

Some states allow homeschoolers to participate in sports at public schools. These rules vary, and the best thing to do is to check with your local school district. Some private schools will also let homeschoolers play on their sports teams. For example, my kids played basketball and volleyball at the private Christian school that maintained our records during their middle school years.

Our city also has a homeschool sports league that offers basketball, volleyball, soccer, ultimate frisbee, cross country, and track. Parents and homeschool alumni started it and now manage the different teams. My son and daughter have played basketball, ultimate frisbee, and volleyball through this group while in high school. They've played against homeschool teams from nearby towns, private Christian schools, and some small public schools. Last year they had eighty kids come out for ultimate frisbee, so they started their own league, and the six teams played each other.

If you don't have these opportunities in your community, think about starting something. It's been great for my kids to be on non-academic teams. They've made friends and had amazing fun. And for those students who want to compete at a higher level, participation in AAU sports is always an option.

Online Schools

We have close friends who put all three of their girls through online public high school. This option will vary by state. While this is technically not homeschooling, their girls were welcome to take co-op classes and join homeschool sports and academic teams in our area. There are also online schools with no affiliation to the public school system. Some are considered homeschooling, and some are regarded as private schools. Regardless, they are good options if you want your children to be home but don't want to be solely responsible for their education. Accreditation of these programs may provide some assurance of quality, but in most states is not legally required. Some of these programs are free and can be excellent cost-effective solutions. However, the disadvantages are the same as those of a public or private school. They can be a one-size-fits-all approach to educating.

HOW DO I DO THIS?

O nce you've chosen curriculums and any outside classes or activities for your child, you need to start thinking about how you will homeschool on a day-to-day basis. How do you do this? First, you need to have a plan to get through the curriculum in a school year. A well-planned weekly schedule can be a huge factor in meeting that goal. Second, you must ensure your child has learned the material. How you grade their schoolwork and test them (if you choose to do so) can also contribute to successful homeschooling.

Scheduling

Scheduling our school days took trial and error for me to figure out, even with just two children. At the beginning of each school year, I would plan a sample school week for the upcoming semester. I would include every subject for each child, including extracurricular activities. There are several things to ask yourself when doing this.

How many subjects can you schedule in a day for each child? What subjects do you need to do daily, and how much time should you allocate for each one?
The number of subjects you schedule for your children each day depends on the child. Some children will work quicker than others, depending on the subject being taught. My daughter and son typically did six subjects daily, approximately fifteen to thirty

minutes per lesson in early elementary school. Starting in fourth grade, I allowed thirty to sixty minutes per subject because the coursework became more demanding. I scheduled less on Fridays and used those afternoons for make-up work, field trips, or just to end the school week early.

As my kids moved into middle school, I scheduled about four subjects daily and allowed one to two hours per lesson. And in high school, they did approximately two to three subjects per day. However, keep in mind that there was no homework involved. They finished everything assigned during that time. This approach is a different way of thinking from a public school where students complete much of the work at home in the evenings. Extracurriculars can sometimes affect the schedule too. For example, there are countless music lessons going on and competition teams meeting during any given school day for many homeschoolers.

After you've chosen your curriculum, look at the total number of lessons for each subject and divide that in half. This tells you how many lessons your child will need to complete each semester.

Example: Grammar textbook - 54 lessons total
                 54/2 semesters = 27 lessons per semester

Next, look at the calendar and count how many weeks you realistically expect to homeschool for the year. (We always took time off for fall and spring breaks, a week at Thanksgiving, and a few weeks off at Christmas.) Once you know how many weeks you will have each semester, divide that number into the number of lessons. For example, we typically school for 18 weeks, five days a week in the first semester.

Example: 27 lessons per semester
                 27/18weeks = 1.5 lessons/week

The next step is to look at the lesson plans for each subject. For example, is each lesson designed to be done in one sitting? If so, in the example above, you might want to schedule two days and plan to get two lessons done each week and finish the subject early, either in the semester or for the whole year. Or, if this is a subject your child struggles with, you may need to schedule several days for each lesson and just know that you may have to allow extra time at the end of the year to finish the curriculum or pick up where you left off at the start of the next school year.

For some subjects, multiple days are usually expected to finish a lesson. For example, you might teach the lesson one day, assign and grade work over the next two to three days, and then have your child take a test on the material or turn in a writing assignment at the end of the week. Doing this would require the subject to be scheduled four to five days a week.

Most teachers' manuals will suggest how to teach the lessons to get through all the material in a school year. Look at these closely when making your schedule. If you choose an all-in-one curriculum, this planning will already be done for you.

Sometimes your child will struggle with certain learning concepts and sail through others. That's perfectly normal. Remember, the goal is to ensure your child understands the information to the best of their ability before moving on to the next lesson. If that takes longer than you had planned, that's okay. On the other hand, if you have a child that flies through their schoolwork and does well, then let them fly and adjust the schedule accordingly. You oversee the learning and scheduling and can plan what you think is best for each child.

Lastly, schedules will most likely need adjustments as you move through the school year. All this will take trial and error so remember that nothing is set in stone. Basically, a schedule will show you how many lessons your children need to complete each week to finish the curriculum for each subject by the end of the school year and how much you plan to accomplish weekly to work toward that goal. Doing this propelled me on during the days and weeks when I wanted to slack off. I'd be lying if I said that still didn't happen occasionally. But, knowing in the back of my mind exactly how much we needed to get done each week in order to take the summer off always kept us moving forward. It became a form of indirect accountability for me.

What will make each day flow more smoothly?
Take some time to think about what will make your days flow as smoothly as possible. If you know your kids have difficulty waking up, schedule a subject they enjoy first thing in the morning. Or you can prepare a class that everyone can do together to help start the day. If you have a child that doesn't like math and draws out an assignment for hours, schedule that last. They may speed it up when they see that their siblings have finished for the afternoon. You know your children better than anyone else; plan your days with their personalities in mind. Again, homeschooling can be a highly tailored education for every student - not just the curriculum but also the schedule. Remember, the goal is to help your child build a solid educational foundation, not to mimic public school.

What subjects can your children do together?
When my daughter started kindergarten, my son was three years old. He was more than interested in what we were doing, so I included him in everything I could. He joined in art lessons, simple science experiments, history stories, and my reading chapter books aloud to them. He still wanted to be included when my daughter started first grade, so I ordered him a kindergarten math book and a handwriting workbook and let him participate in almost everything we did. I had once read to "teach to the oldest, and the others will come along," and because I didn't know what I was doing at this point, I took that advice and ran with it. Doing this has benefitted my son greatly over the years. He's been slightly ahead in his classes, which has given him confidence in his ability to learn and has led to a love of learning. I would not have made him do school with us if he had not shown interest in keeping up with his sister at such an early age. It was always an option for him. (Note: The handwriting book proved very unpopular and was put up for a few years until he was ready.)

With scheduling, I recommend if you're teaching multiple kids at home, find curriculums for a few subjects that you can teach everyone at the same time and choose age-appropriate assignments for each child. Charlotte Mason or classical curriculums can make this easier. I found this was fun to do with history and science. For history, we used *The Story of the World* series by Susan Wise Bauer and Jessie Wise. For science, we used Nancy Larson® Science. Both were easy to adapt and teach to more than one child at a time. New curriculums come out all the time, which is why you need to do your research and determine what will be the best fit for your family.

Where do extracurricular activities fit into the schedule?

Extracurricular activities fit into the schedule wherever you can find room. For example, my daughter's violin teacher would only schedule lessons for homeschoolers during the school day. Some years my kids spent almost every Friday at Science Olympiad and Science Bowl practices. In middle school, we would leave our house around 2:15 p.m. daily to get to sports practices. All these things cut into the school day. Yes, most of them can still be counted as school hours, but that doesn't mean that your kids have any less schoolwork that needs to be completed. My advice is to pick and choose wisely. Make sure the extracurriculars are worth the time spent doing them.

What about interruptions in our day, such as doctor's appointments, playdates, and other disruptors?

Life happens. There will be things you have to do and things you'd rather do. Of course, it's best to have as few disruptions as possible, but that's not always realistic. That's why having a schedule is important. You'll know when to rein in the distractions if you see that you're getting a few weeks behind in certain subjects.

Should I use a homeschool planner?

I started homeschooling kindergarten using an online calendar. It was legible and organized, but it took too long to enter everything and make changes. I later switched to store-bought teacher's planners for a few years and wrote in them with a pencil. Doing this worked fine, but I wanted something more tailored to our needs, so I finally designed my own with Excel. Many online companies now create customized teacher's planners, online or hard copy. The samples I've included below simply show you what worked for us.

Week of				KATHERINE	NATHAN			
Time	Monday		Time	Tuesday		Time	Wednesday	

7.1 Weekly Schedule Template 2-Student Alternating

Figure 7.1 shows a left page of my open planner. It has a space for the date and columns for each day of the week next to narrower columns to write in times during the day. The spaces in each column are color-coded for each child, enabling me to quickly glance to see what my son or daughter should be doing at any given time. The larger area below is for extracurricular activities after school hours, and the bottom space is for dinner plans.

7.2 Weekly Schedule Template 2-Student Block

Figure 7.2 is an example of what I used as my kids got older. Since they were doing fewer subjects together and had more classes outside the home, it was easier to have larger spaces to record all their daily assignments in one place. This design might also be better for homeschooling more than two or three children.

I have one friend who homeschools five kids and carries a small pocket calendar in her purse. In that calendar, every six weeks, she has marked what lesson each child should be on in their different subjects and adjusts if they are behind schedule. That works for them, and her kids are doing great. Unfortunately,

I'm not disciplined enough to use that method. You'll need to experiment and find what makes your homeschooling work well. Figuring this out took me a few years.

I've included in Appendix B a weekly schedule sample for the first semester of my daughter's seventh and my son's fifth-grade school year. I would try to follow this as I made each week's schedule throughout the semester. If our week was scheduled out, it was productive. If I didn't have a plan, it was like herding cats all week, of which I, too, was one.

When my daughter started high school, I kept doing a weekly schedule. By tenth grade, I began pulling back, and for eleventh and twelfth grade, she needed to make her own for the week and show it to me. In preparation for college, she needed to start taking responsibility for her time management. It was hard to watch some weeks, but she learned from her mistakes, and we both think that helped her navigate her first year of college with less stress.

One last note about scheduling: You'll notice on the sample schedule that we didn't start our school day until 9:00 a.m. We're not early morning people. One homeschooling family I know doesn't get started until 11:00 a.m. each day. They feel like they learn better by starting later. The choice is yours. I had a friend tell me once that she had heard homeschooled kids have trouble making it to 8:00 a.m. classes when they get to college. I laughed and told her that was silly – that I attended public school, kindergarten through twelfth grade, and hardly ever made it to my 8:00 a.m. college classes. That may have more to do with your personality and social activities than being homeschooled. But, again, do what you think is best for your family.

Grading

First, you must ensure your grading system follows your state's guidelines if there are any. I have found that grading is what I like the least about homeschooling. However, it's extremely important to grade your child's work and do it promptly. You cannot sit down and grade three months of math at one time and expect your child to make corrections on what they did twenty lessons ago. To make it a little easier on myself, we would occasionally have "participation classes." If my kids did their best and completed the activities or assignments, I gave them an A. However, I do not recommend doing this for core subjects like math, grammar, composition, or science. For math, I would grade my kids' work and then let them go back and correct what they missed. I gave them all the points if they were right the second time. I did this with most subjects. Our goal was to master the material. If they achieved that, they got an A. I used yearly testing to back up their grades. You cannot give your kid straight A's and then have them score below grade level on their testing. That will and should raise a red flag. If your yearly testing does not at least mildly reflect your child's grades, you may need to consider that your child isn't grasping all the information as well as you had thought.

Testing

I realize the importance put on testing has become out of control over the past few decades in many school systems. In some places, there's more test prep than actual learning. It is my opinion, however, NOT to shy away from end-of-year testing. Yes, it's easier not to test. And, yes, it's a lot of pressure for the homeschooling parent and, often, the child. But I would recommend testing for a few reasons.

The first is that testing helped guide our curriculum choices. For example, my daughter tested significantly lower in spelling than in other subjects in the first, second, and third grades. We gave the spelling curriculum she was using a good shot, but she was struggling and wasn't a natural speller. In fact, her test scores were higher than I had anticipated based on the work she was doing at home. To make matters worse, she would ask me why something was spelled a certain way, and my best answer was, "That's just the way it's spelled, Sweetie." It clearly wasn't working for us.

I researched spelling curriculums that summer after she completed the third grade and decided on a different one to start the next school year. I had passed it up a few years earlier because it looked like a lot of work for me to teach. However, it turned out to be excellent and worth the extra effort. I could teach my daughter and son the lessons simultaneously and simply adjust the assignments to make them on his grade level. This curriculum also answered all my daughter's "why" questions. Finally, spelling started to make sense to her. That year, she scored in the 95th percentile and stayed there until she aged out of testing. So, I've used yearly testing to guide my curriculum choices through the years and to determine if there was a subject on which we needed to spend more time.

Is testing a perfect system? Of course not. But there is another reason I recommend testing. It's so your children will become comfortable doing it. I would tell my kids before they tested that all they needed to do was try their best on each question. That was all I asked of them. I told them that doing their best helped me choose good curriculums for them. There was absolutely no need to tie it to their grades or make them nervous about it. In most states, the only people who see the results are the parents and the administrators of your homeschooling records. However, your kids need to be comfortable taking tests because their lives will be full of them – even for basic things like a driver's license.

For example, I had no idea when I was young that I would one day go to optometry school. Each class had a midterm and a final. Those two tests, which often had only fifty multiple-choice questions yet covered volumes of material, determined whether I passed or failed a class. These classes were sending me into six-figure student loan debt that I wouldn't be able to pay back without this degree. See where I'm going with this? Most people aren't going to optometry school, but if your child wants to further their education one day or advance in their career, they need to be practiced and comfortable taking tests.

With homeschooling, the benefit of test-taking, especially in the elementary years, is that it doesn't have any strings attached. It's not tied to how much money a school will receive or a teacher's evaluation or salary. Testing is strictly for the parent to guide the homeschooling. No one even needs to see it but you. And this includes extended family.

I know testing is a contentious subject for many people. These are my opinions and the reasons for them. If you don't agree, then don't agree. You're the parent. You're in charge. If you feel strongly about not testing, then don't do it if that's something your state allows. No one homeschools the same way. We all bring our personal opinions, often based on past experiences and the temperament of each child we teach, into the equation. This makes it a little different for everyone.

HOW DO I HOMESCHOOL ELEMENTARY SCHOOL?

O nce my husband and I had committed to homeschooling, I began telling others. It seemed hard for some people to keep the "you've lost your mind" look off their faces. Some outright said to me that I would ruin my kids. Both my dad and my sister strongly disagreed with our decision. My dad even told me that the schools would win if I decided to homeschool. I responded by telling him that the schools would lose if I homeschooled because they wouldn't get my well-behaved kids or their minds. There are some things in my life that I deeply care about what people think, but thankfully this wasn't one of them. I had spent four years in college and four years in optometry school. I thought I could surely teach kindergarten. So, we moved forward with excitement.

I looked at several kindergarten curriculums, but they all seemed too easy and not worth the money. Between two years of preschool and working with my daughter at home, she was already reading and counting. So I decided to start with the book *What Your Kindergartener Needs to Know* by E.D. Hirsch Jr. and

John Holden. We did a few sections on different subjects each day. Usually, we were finished within a few hours and then would bake or play for the rest of the required school day. I liked this because my young son could also participate in our activities. At this time, I was still working part-time (Thursdays and Saturdays), and my in-laws had agreed to homeschool on Thursdays. So I usually saved crafts and field trips for that day. For example, one of the art sections in the book talked about sculptures, so I planned a field trip for them to walk around downtown with their grandparents, look at the various statues, and take pictures. That was a fun day that became one of their childhood memories.

We finished that book by December, and I decided to start first grade curriculum after the holidays. I purchased the book *The Well-trained Mind; A Guide to Classical Education at Home* by Susan Wise Bauer and Jessie Wise and decided to follow the authors' guidelines for homeschooling. Even though we eventually ended up doing our own thing, this helped me feel confident about what I was doing in the beginning. After all, it had worked for them.

As I look back on that first year, homeschooling was a true blessing. Rather than working full-time to afford private school for my daughter and daycare for my son, I was able to be home with my kids and watch them learn, laugh, and play. I almost liked being home with them better than before we started homeschooling. Our days had purpose and structure in the mornings, and I liked that.

One thing that bothered me, though, was that we were alone. We had friends but not homeschooled friends, so I joined a Facebook group and started connecting with others. Doing this was a labor of love. I could easily be a hermit and be happy, but I knew my kids would need friends to go on field trips and play with during the school year.

In the various online homeschool groups, different mothers would post playdates, usually at local parks, and invite "friends" to join them. It became obvious that we were not alone in feeling lonely. We went on playdate after playdate with strangers. My kids were shy. Most of the moms were fine, but we never really clicked with anyone. We needed more consistency than this, and by the time my daughter began third grade, we had found what we were looking for: PE at the YMCA.

Our local YMCA had started a homeschool PE class for kindergarten through sixth grade. The kids were divided into older and younger groups and did one hour of swimming and one hour of instructional PE on Tuesday and Thursday mornings. Parents were encouraged to leave, but I stayed the first few times. My kids weren't strong swimmers, and that concerned me. I also wanted to see how the other kids behaved. And if I'm being completely honest, I wanted to ensure my kids were being treated well. After watching them swim in three PE classes, I realized that I was the one who may have been holding them back in the pool. They were playing and having fun and seemed in good hands, so I left. Those classes saved us. My kids made friends, and I made friends. We went to amusement parks, playgrounds, and on field trips together. We stayed there and took classes for three years.

When my son was in late elementary, I decided it was time to try a homeschool co-op. Up to this point, I had taught all core subjects in-house, but it was now time to delegate a few classes. During our time at this co-op, I was a parent volunteer in art, high school chemistry, and elementary theater classes. I noticed some kids were sweet and well-behaved, some were too cool to be there, and others were a bit nerdy. It was a similar cross-section to what you might see at your local public school. There were kids I encouraged mine to hang out with and others I told them not to go near. I later found out there were drug problems, questionable teachers, and many of the same issues that are prevalent at public schools. The difference was this was only one day a week, I could pick and choose the classes, and if we decided it wasn't for us, we could leave.

Looking back, homeschooling through the elementary years was a lot of work, but equally fun and rewarding. Those years created some of our fondest memories.

Appendix C shows a list of our favorite curriculums we used during that time, as well as what we liked the most in middle and high school. Again, every family is different and I'm not recommending you repeat or use exactly what we did. I just wanted to share with you a few of the curriculums that were special to us.

Elementary School Tips

A parent needs to be at home.
I realize everyone has different circumstances, but if possible, one parent needs to be at home and primarily responsible for homeschooling. You can delegate some teaching to friends, grandparents, or co-ops, but homeschooling is a parental responsibility. I quit my part-time job when my daughter started fourth grade. As I mentioned, my in-laws had been helping us out and homeschooling on the days I worked. And while they were happy to do this, I realized it wasn't fair to them. They had to crack down on my kids as the curriculum got harder and make them do their schoolwork. They weren't getting to enjoy being grandparents.

On the other hand, my mother homeschooled my nephew in the seventh and eighth grades. He didn't want to do his work, and she had trouble making him do it. She was used to being the fun-loving grandmother and let him get by with things she shouldn't have. When he returned to school in ninth grade, he struggled academically and barely graduated from high school. It takes a parent (or primary guardian) to be "all in" on the homeschooling.

However, having a parent at home comes at a cost for most families. For several years after I quit working, I was on the tightest budget of my life. Every penny was accounted for. I gave up a career and a second income. Looking back, I have no regrets.

You will have good days and bad days.
The bad days (or weeks) don't make you a lousy homeschooling parent. Your kids aren't doomed. It's normal. Trust me!

Consistency is important.

My kids knew that by 9:00 a.m., they would be doing school. Period. Understanding this at a young age will make the middle school and high school years much easier.

Planning is necessary.

It's easy to let the days and weeks get away from you if you don't have a plan. When my kids were in kindergarten through ninth grade, I tried to sit down every Sunday for an hour or two and plan the upcoming week. There were many weeks that we didn't get through everything I had scheduled, so I would circle the assignments in my planner and then work them into the following week. Again, I can't stress enough the importance of planning. It may be the single most important thing that has made our homeschooling successful. I wouldn't recommend "winging it" on a regular basis. That's just a way to get by, not a way to excel. Your kids deserve the best you can do.

Like many, my kids and I are usually burned out by the end of the school year. With planning, we typically finish up by the end of May. It has always been important to me that we have a summer break comparable to public and private schools in the area. I've never wanted my kids to miss out on this because of being homeschooled. I've always felt, as their teacher and administrator, that no matter how challenging the schoolwork is or how difficult my child is behaving (see more in the middle school section), it's ultimately my responsibility to get them through the material by the end of May so we can have a few months off in the summer.

One family we know has seven kids. They simply need more time each week to do laundry, grocery shop, and schedule appointments, so they take every Friday off but homeschool year-round. Doing this works great for them. Homeschooling offers them the flexibility that works best for their family. One year I decided that we would start school in July and take the entire five weeks off between Thanksgiving and New Year's Day. We only did that once. None of us thought it was worth missing out on a month of summer. Plan what you think will work best for your situation, and then adjust accordingly over time to make it better.

Continuity is important.

As mentioned, switching curriculums every month, semester, or year can potentially leave gaps in your child's education, mainly in the subjects that build from year to year, like math and grammar. Sometimes changing the curriculum is necessary, but thoroughly research and try to choose wisely the first time. Over time, this will benefit your child and your pocketbook.

Don't overschedule.

Overscheduling was a hard lesson for us to learn in every phase of our homeschooling. In the younger grades, it was field trips and play dates. Sports and competition teams like Science Olympiad took most of our time as they got older. As we got more involved in the homeschooling community, it became clear that we could be busy every day with field trips, co-ops, or special events. Everything seemed worthy in some way. Know that it's okay to say no to good opportunities. Your children will not suffer socially. However, they will suffer if they can't read. So, my advice is to pick and choose what activities are best for your kids and you as a parent. A tired, cranky family isn't the goal here.

Socializing your child is not a problem.

Socialization seems to be a grave concern for friends, family, teachers, and even strangers who don't think you should homeschool your kids. However, there are so many opportunities available to homeschoolers, as discussed previously, that socializing your children is relatively easy if you're willing to leave your house and make an effort.

Ironically, a friend of mine that homeschools said she pulled her three kids out of public school because of the socialization. According to her, her children were learning bad habits and bad words the few times during the school day they were allowed to talk and be social. She found homeschooling was a far better way for her kids to engage with others.

Don't underestimate the power of a bribe.
I wouldn't recommend this daily or even weekly, but the power of a small toy sitting on top of the refrigerator can go a long way in motivating young children to complete their work. Who doesn't want to be rewarded? Sometimes I did this when my kids finished a workbook or, as I mentioned earlier, when they learned the multiplication tables. But I also randomly surprised them because they were doing what I asked of them and trying their best. I did this less in middle school and not at all in high school. As my kids got older, I wanted them to know that they needed to complete their work because it was assigned, not because they would get paid or receive a gift for doing it.

Have fun!
Yes, there is work to be done, but who says learning can't be fun? Some of this requires planning. You can read about how the earth revolves around the sun, or you can set up a lamp on your dining room table and demonstrate it with your young children. You can read about famous artists and then surprise your kids with an afternoon trip to the local art museum. One year on leap day, a friend of mine drove her kids to Sonic and told them they could only order dessert for lunch. That day they learned that leap day was special because it only occurs once every four years. I remember volunteering to take dinner to a new mom one day. I'm a below-average cook. Six hours and two trips to the grocery store later, we delivered the food. My kids thought it was fun. When they asked me about doing school, I told them they had learned about helping others that day. They high-fived each other in the back seat.

Occasionally, when my kids were young, I loaded them in the van after a rough morning of homeschooling and drove them past the local elementary. If I timed it just right, the students were lined up on the playground, waiting to go back inside the building for the afternoon. I would say, "That could be you, but you're already finished for the day," and then we would drive to Chickfil-A. We all need some fun and a fresh perspective every now and then.

Homeschooling is a great family lifestyle.
I can't emphasize this enough. Your kids get their work done during the day. Evenings are for sports, family activities, etc. Schedule lighter if you have a lot coming up during a particular week. You're in control of that. School also doesn't limit your travel. Take spring break in February if you want to. Don't take any breaks and finish in April. Take every Friday off. You're in charge of the calendar. If you meet the required number of school days for the year, the choice is yours in most states. The flexibility of homeschooling makes it a great lifestyle choice for so many families.

HOW DO I HOMESCHOOL MIDDLE SCHOOL?

O nce my kids got into middle school, the years started to fly. The school that maintained our records was a small private Christian school that invited homeschoolers to participate in their team sports. My daughter joined the volleyball team, and my son joined the basketball team. Daily practices were required unless there was a game. My kids also became eligible to compete in academic competitions during these years. They both were taking music lessons and my daughter played in an orchestra. In addition, they were getting more involved in our co-op and church youth group. And lastly, our church now had several homeschooling families, so a few moms started a monthly book club and a field trip group so our kids could get together outside of church services during the week. We were overcommitted before I ever saw it coming.

Everything also got harder to teach in middle school. The curriculum was more challenging, and the assignments were longer. That, combined with all our extracurricular activities, made for some stressful times. I longed for the sweet days of elementary school.

My husband would usually call to check in a few mornings a

week. A typical scenario would be my daughter and I starting on our third hour of math. I'm angry, and she's crying. Thankfully, my son liked math. His kryptonite was writing. Even a short paragraph assignment would produce tears and a dramatic fall to the floor. During this time, the good and bad days started to even out for us. But we kept on going, and little by little, my kids realized they would have to do the work anyway, so it was better to try their best and get it done. This awakening didn't happen overnight, though.

In middle school, I came up with a motto for our homeschooling: "Question everything but find the answer." I felt that too much groupthink was happening in TV shows, on social media, and in brick-and-mortar schools. I wanted my kids to be able to think for themselves and to think critically. Intellectual curiosity is important.

Also, from day one, I wanted my children to love to learn. Growing up, I could memorize large amounts of material long enough to take a test but never really knew the information. It wasn't until my second year of optometry school that I learned how to learn. Until then, I had never felt like I had the time to dive deep and understand the information being tested. I thought it was too important to make a good grade on the test, so I memorized everything and spit it back out. I never really loved to learn and didn't want that for my kids.

Yes, they tested at the end of each school year, but as I've said, that was more about guiding our curriculum and seeing where we might need to spend more time. I never wanted testing in the different subjects throughout the school years to trump learning the material, so I adjusted my grading accordingly. For some subjects, assignments were worth much more than tests. And for others, participation was all that I required. For example, when my daughter was in eighth grade and my son was in sixth, I ordered an engineering video series from The Great Courses and added it to our science curriculum. We watched it for an hour three days a week that entire winter. I told my kids that if they stayed awake and answered a few questions about what we had just watched, they would get A's. A West Point professor taught the video, and by the time we finished, all three of us had significantly increased our knowledge of the world around us. We learned about the different wires on telephone poles and why roads slant downward on the sides. We learned the engineering involved in building a house, cellphone technology, and how the simple machines work in our home. After that video series, my son decided he wanted to be an engineer.

The middle school years are great for the exploration of different areas of study. As I've mentioned, we joined a Science Bowl and Science Olympiad team mainly to expose the kids to multiple areas of science. They competed with homemade musical instruments they had to be able to tune. They learned about thermodynamics and even built a model roller coaster based on scientific principles.

During this time, they also took theater and art classes at their co-op. They both took music lessons and were involved in sports. My desire for them to try different things and get to know themselves better during these years had pros and cons. They were exposed to some great stuff, and both found definite interests. But we were also overcommitted, and life was crazy. It was too much some days. We remedied that in high school, and I'll tell you how in the next chapter.

Looking back, during my kids' middle school years, Common Core had a lot to do with the growth of homeschoolers at our church and in our city. I had read a few things about it and heard that parents were upset, but I never really had to investigate it further. Instead, I simply chose the curriculum I thought would be best for us, so Common Core was never an issue.

We also felt profound sadness during the school shootings that happened during that time. I was thankful I never had to consider the safety of my kids at school. It was peace of mind that I didn't take for granted.

And lastly, throughout our homeschooling years, my children's education was rarely interrupted. If the schools shut down for a week due to the flu or inclement weather, we continued working. More importantly, nothing changed for us when most public schools transitioned to online learning during the COVID-19 pandemic. My kids continued to learn at the same pace they always had.

Middle School Tips

Your children will test you during this time.
If they cry, pout, roll their eyes or throw themselves on the floor, remain calm and remind them that they still must complete their assignments. Make them aware that they may have to miss out on a sports practice or free time to do it. Your kids need to know you're serious about this, and you need to follow through. If you're consistent, they'll eventually get the message (some take longer than others), but it will benefit your homeschooling through high school. Remember, YOU are in charge.

You may just choose to overcommit during these years.
Each parent must decide what is best for their family. We were so busy during this time that life became crazy, and the years flew by. I was spending hours in my car waiting for my kids during their practices or rehearsals. In fact, on any given day, you could find me sleeping on the third-row seat of my minivan. I was exhausted and bored at the same time. It was a labor of love for my kids, for sure.

However, this was a great time to get our kids involved in different things so they could start to see where their interests lie and what some of their strengths might be, which is why we continued to be somewhat overcommitted. These experiences exposed my kids to new ideas and priorities and greatly influenced how we homeschooled high school.

Middle school is an awkward time for every kid, not just homeschoolers.
You may disagree with me, but sometimes the homeschool mom must be the "mean kid on the bus", but in a much more loving way. My daughter would get ready to go somewhere and come downstairs looking like she had done nothing to herself except

put on her glasses. Hair frizzy, questionable teeth brushing, wrinkled clothes, slumped over. Uh, no. I would have her go back upstairs and try again and again until she met the minimum threshold of what I thought was acceptable.

Let me pause to say that I would never criticize my kids for something they couldn't change. I know people who had parents that made fun of their noses or acne. A relative once told me my feet weren't pretty enough to wear sandals. I would never do that to my kids. But things they can put a little more effort into to look presentable? You bet. Brush your teeth, brush your hair, wear clothes that fit you, wash your face, stand up straight, and use deodorant. Middle school is the time to learn these things and develop good habits. How you present yourself matters whether people want to admit that or not. An awkward homeschooled child could look very similar to a public-schooled child but be called out for not being socialized enough. Sadly, that's still the perception of homeschooling in many people's minds.

Middle school is when a lot of homeschool moms burn out.

Let's face it. In middle school, you're no longer doing cute crafts with your kids and counting that hour you baked cookies as part of the school day. The curriculum gets more challenging and demanding of your time. That, combined with extracurricular activities, preteen attitudes, and social issues, is a recipe for burnout. One day, I was volunteering in a co-op class, and the instructor was a retired public-school teacher who had now taught homeschoolers for about seven years. I told her my daughter was starting high school the following year, and she asked if she could give me some advice. She told me that she had seen a pattern in the homeschooling community that hurts the kids as they get older. The parents are very active through eighth grade and then are hardly involved when the kids get to high school because they expect them to be more independent. She attributed this to burnout and unrealistic expectations for their homeschoolers. She said she'd had top students in middle school barely get a high school education, which affected what they could do after they graduated. She completely stepped on my toes. Throughout my daughter's eighth-grade year, I had been thinking, "Okay, if we can get through this year, next year she'll be in high school, and I won't have to do very much." That was my plan. This teacher crushed it, and I'm glad she did. You really can't expect your 15-year-old, who can't even drive yet, to do high school by themselves. I ended up going "all in" my daughter's freshman year, and that backfired too, which I'll discuss in the next chapter.

You can continue to instill your family's values on deeper topics or issues that arise during these years.
This season of life goes by fast. I love that I homeschooled my kids during their middle school years. They started asking me questions about sex, politics, and other things on their minds. It was great to have those conversations, and it established a pattern that they could ask me anything, and I would give them an honest answer. One day, a Viagra commercial came on the radio when my daughter was in the car. She asked what it was (we had already had the sex talk), and I told her. She was utterly grossed out, but at that point, she knew she could talk to me about anything, and she has over the years.

Homeschooling has presented many opportunities to teach our children our family values and about life in general. Whether something comes up in a science lesson or they have questions about something they've heard on TV, they are learning from their parents. They're not getting information from some misguided kid in their class or from a teacher who has an entirely different set of values than we have. By showing your kids you care about what they are learning and that you're willing to answer any question they ask, you can build trust and closeness during these years that will hopefully last a lifetime.

HOW DO I HOMESCHOOL HIGH SCHOOL?

High school is a whole different animal. Much of the flexibility you've enjoyed in elementary and middle school goes away. But not all of it. Remember, you are the parent and are still making the decisions. By flexibility, I mean that most states require students to pass a specific number of classes before graduating. Also, if your child plans to attend college, certain high-school credits are required for admission to most universities. What is needed can vary. For example, state universities typically require two high school foreign language credits, while more elite schools may require four. This information is available on most university websites. Knowing this early on can help you plan the high school years more effectively.

I took the co-op teacher's words to heart and, although slightly burned out, planned out my daughter's entire freshman year of high school. I had decided to teach all her academic classes at home. One reason was that, as with public and private schools, you'll find that some of the homeschool co-op teachers are just okay, not great, and I didn't want her to have high school classes that weren't worth the time and money. At least at home,

I could provide her with a good curriculum and strong learning objectives. She still attended our co-op, but mostly for fun classes like ballroom dance, theater, choir, and to see her friends.

Unfortunately, my plan didn't turn out as well as I had imagined. To give my daughter a strong start in high school, I had chosen a challenging curriculum for every subject. What could go wrong with that? A lot. One month into the first semester, we were both miserable. The poor child was writing several papers a week for English, in addition to taking geometry, introduction to number theory, biology, Spanish, speech, music appreciation, and PE. It was all too much. That year, I learned a hard lesson at my daughter's expense and realized that not all classes need to be "hard-core."

The example above is why it's important to provide exposure opportunities for your kids in middle school and high school so they can start learning what their strengths are and where their interests lie. For example, my daughter took a computer programming class in middle school and enjoyed it. She understood it quickly, and her dad and I saw she was becoming increasingly interested in computers and seemed to have an aptitude for programming. More importantly, she mentioned that she might like to do that as a job one day. I decided after her freshman year to focus more on STEM (Science, Technology, Engineering, and Mathematics) classes the next school year and make the other required courses easier. We knew she didn't particularly enjoy history by this time, so why make that class difficult? Time is precious. If she had loved history and wanted to teach it one day, that would have been a different story. I would have found her the best and richest history curriculum or instruction I could afford, and we would have continued strongly down that path. I don't want to minimize the importance of studying history or any other subject, for that matter. My point is that there are other activities for your high school student outside of classwork, such as learning to drive, getting a part-time job, social activities, or sports. There's not enough time in the day to make every class advanced, so it made sense for us to start focusing on my kids' strengths and interests. I felt this would benefit their future the most.

By the end of my daughter's sophomore year, she was convinced she wanted to attend college and major in computer science. So that next fall, I enrolled her in a nearby community college for Computer 101, a class that taught basic computer programming. In college, I went through three different majors before I decided to attend optometry school. Doing this cost me time and money, so I wanted her to dive in a little deeper to see if this was something she truly liked. We did this her junior year because if she didn't like computer science as much as she thought she would, we would have her senior year to explore other interests.

She loved the class, so we started to look for more opportunities. She took a second computer class at the community college the following semester. During her junior year, she also joined a CyberPatriot team and, from that point on, was hooked on cybersecurity, which is what she went on to study in college.

During my daughter's sophomore year, we encouraged her to try different activities. Her dad and I told her she would take a break from violin and orchestra for one year. It was too time-consuming and expensive, considering I had to make her practice every week. She had begun playing at age five. It started as a fifteen-minute lesson and was thirty-five dollars a month, including the violin rental. Fast forward ten years, and it's an entirely different story. My daughter was no longer enjoying the music, and all of this was now costing me the equivalent of a used car payment every month. The previous week, between orchestra rehearsal, lessons, and a violin competition, I had waited in the car for her for eight hours over a twenty-four-hour period. I finally said to my husband, "Why are we doing this? This is crazy."

I also wanted her to have the opportunity to try other things, and there just wasn't enough time in a day to do everything. She cried when my husband and I told her she was going to take a break and that we would re-evaluate in one year. However, two months later, she joined a volleyball team through a local private school and never looked back. It gave her exactly what she needed at the time - new friends and exercise. She was happy.

We learned from this that if something truly isn't working, it's not worth it. Did we disappoint the grandparents that we pulled her out of violin? Probably. Did we make her violin teacher mad? Yes. Did her violin teacher think we were ruining her chances of a college scholarship to study violin? Yes. But we did it anyway. We did what we thought was best for our daughter, and it turned out to be just that. She went on to play volleyball, be more involved with our church youth group, and hang out with friends. She still picks up her violin and plays, but now she enjoys it.

My son is two years younger than my daughter, and I must admit, he has received a slightly better education. I've made most of my mistakes with her. Despite much research, sometimes a curriculum just isn't as good as you think it will be. He's benefited from his sister having to do everything first. His experience with Science Olympiad starting in middle school and his deep understanding of math has led him down a STEM pathway also. This past year he decided he would like to study aerospace engineering in college. We've started visiting universities with strong engineering programs. We've also found local aerospace engineers that he can talk to and ask questions about the profession.

Initially, the thought of homeschooling high school was intimidating. During elementary school, my husband, the kids, and I reassessed yearly to determine if this was still what was best for each of them and our family. When my daughter entered middle school, we committed to the entire three years. Middle school can be challenging, and we didn't think it would be wise to enroll her right in the middle of it. When she started high school, we gave her the option to continue homeschooling, attend private school, or enroll in public school. My daughter wasn't sure what she wanted to do, so we researched and visited some of her options. After investigating, she decided she wanted to continue being homeschooled. Two years later, my son was offered the same options and also chose to homeschool. However, we did not commit to the entire four years for either of them. High school needs to prepare your child for what comes next, whether it's college, a full-time job, an apprenticeship, or a trade school. If at any time during high school, I felt either of my kids wasn't getting the education they needed for that next step in life, I wanted to keep our options open to find a better place for them to learn.

Now that my daughter has graduated and my son is a senior, I can look back and see that high school is not all that different from the previous grades. Yes, there is a little more accountability, but I've realized that my husband and I (and grandparents, to an extent) are the only adults who genuinely care that my kids are learning. Seriously. No one in any official capacity seems all that concerned about my kids' education. Sure, we're accountable to the private school and the counselor that keeps our records there but only to their lowest standards for graduating. I'm still the one who must prepare my kids for life after graduation. I'm the one that's ultimately responsible for their education. Because of that, I feel free to plan high school in a way that will benefit each of my children the most while still meeting the state-mandated requirements. As I've said before, homeschooling can be a highly tailored education that can well-prepare your children for their future. They can't do this on their own, though. They still need you to guide them and plan their high school years.

High School Tips

Seek Counseling.
I ask a lot of questions. In fact, my family has been known to call me "Captain Question" on field trips and tours. Most of what I've learned and applied to our homeschooling over the years has come from more experienced homeschooling moms. I listen carefully to what has worked, what hasn't worked, what co-op classes are the best, which curriculums they've liked, etc. We also homeschool through a private school that provides a fantastic counselor. If I'm unsure whether to count a class as standard, honors, or AP,

he helps me make that decision. If I need an official transcript sent to a university, he takes care of it. He has written letters of recommendation for both of my children. He is very good at what he does and is available five days a week, year-round. If you don't have access to a good school counselor, ask your questions to fellow homeschooling parents and those that have children in public and private schools.

I have been amazed at the educational opportunities I would have never known about had I not networked with other parents. One night, I was sitting at a volleyball game when the mom next to me randomly said that Governor's School applications were due in early December. I told her I had no idea what she was talking about. It turns out Governor's Schools are month-long residential summer camps that take place at universities across our state in different areas of study, such as the arts, physics, and business. The application process is competitive and available to all rising juniors and seniors in the state, regardless of where you attend school. College credit can be awarded upon completion of the camp. This mom had already homeschooled and graduated two older children, one of which was accepted to MIT, and had experience that I didn't. To this day, she is the only person who has ever mentioned Governor's School to me. Both of my kids applied and got accepted the summers before their senior years. Talk to people and ask questions, whether it's a school counselor or another parent more experienced than you. Connecting with others can save you time, money, and frustration and help you learn about some great opportunities for your kids.

Variety is good.
We've always had a variety of mediums for our classes. I like to use online instruction, video series classes, traditional textbooks, and co-ops. Online courses have taught my kids how to turn assignments in online and adhere to deadlines. Video series courses have always been used for the classes I make a little easier. They're more for exposure to information, and my kids seem to remember subjects like history better using this

approach. Traditional textbooks are the "meat and potatoes" of our homeschool. We've used these for subjects like math and grammar. Finally, co-op classes allow for social time and learning with their peers. These classes teach kids to be accountable to someone other than the homeschool parent, which I think is important as they get older.

All of this prepares them for college, trade school, or the workplace. Look for classes that are the best fit for your student. We joined a different co-op for high school because I wanted my kids to have a particular English teacher. It was worth the move. Both my son and daughter had her, and she helped them take their writing to the next level and prepare them for college. Do your research. Join local homeschool Facebook groups where you'll find parents with opinions and years of experience that can recommend different mediums for learning. As I recommend with this book, take what you want from those sites or take nothing at all. You know your child best.

Dual enrollment is great.
After geometry, almost all my daughter's and son's math courses have been taken as dual enrollment classes at our local community college. If you're not familiar with dual enrollment, it's a program that most community colleges and universities offer that allows high school students to take college classes and receive both high school and college credit for them. For the student, one huge benefit is that they get a whole year of high school credit in one semester. Another benefit for my son is that he will have all his engineering math out of the way before he goes to college. Of course, we want him to work hard in college, but this will lessen his load so that he can also enjoy it. My daughter had enough dual-enrollment credits and test credits from AP, CLEP, and the ACT exams that she started college as a sophomore. This allowed her to jump right into classes in her field of study without affecting her freshman scholarships.

I still remember looking over the high school requirements for the first time and seeing that four math credits were required to graduate. Then I met a mom whose oldest son had been homeschooled and graduated from a state university in four years with chemical engineering and computer science degrees. This kid was obviously incredibly smart, but how in the world did he graduate with two degrees that can each take four to five years to complete? Dual enrollment is how. Four math credits are required to graduate from high school, but no rule says your child can't take additional math classes and count them as electives. The same applies to other subjects. To get the most out of dual enrollment, I recommend making sure the classes your children take will transfer to their preferred colleges. You can find that information online by searching "transfer credit equivalencies (school name)" using the names of the universities your child is interested in attending.

When my daughter started college last year, I learned another benefit of dual enrollment. Many freshman courses such as chemistry and calculus "weed out" students from their degree programs before they even take the first class in their desired field of study. My daughter had taken several of those classes as a dual enrollment student in high school while still under her parent's guidance. Doing this allowed her to jump right into what she was interested in studying during her first year of college. I sometimes wonder how many students drop out after or during their freshman year because they're struggling in classes that have little to do with what they want to study.

Overall, dual enrollment has been a very efficient way for my kids to earn high school credits that will count toward college. Students are usually required to take the ACT and achieve a minimum score based on the classes they want to take at their chosen community college or university. Our state also offers a grant that pays for some of the classes. Most schools will outline their dual enrollment policies on their website.

Don't forget about AP and CLEP tests.
Homeschoolers can take Advanced Placement (AP) courses. If your child wants to take an AP test without taking the class, that is

also allowed. However, keep in mind that for it to count as a high school credit in most states, they must have a textbook or formal course that teaches the subject.

This is the way that I've approached AP classes: If there is an AP exam that will 1) benefit my child in college, and 2) I think they can learn the subject on an advanced level, we'll consider doing it. Next, I look for a rigorous curriculum - whether it's a textbook, co-op class, or an online AP course. If we decide to proceed, we then sign up through local public or private high schools to take the tests in our area. Not every high school will offer all the AP tests, so you may need to call around, beginning in September, to find a place for your child to take a particular test. (My advice is to be nice to your high school contact and be prompt with your payment. They are sometimes registering hundreds of students. It's always best if homeschoolers aren't their biggest problem.)

Next, I'll research and purchase the best AP study guide I can find on that subject. The study guides are important. They give your child an idea of what they will be tested on, how to take the test, and also provide practice tests. Lastly, it's important to allow enough time at the end of the school year to prepare for the AP exams. In the past, I've allotted two to three weeks before the tests were scheduled to review and work through the study guides. This meant that my daughter or son needed to be finished with the class or curriculum related to each test before then. Take that extra time your child will need into consideration when you're counting the weeks you have in a semester or year to finish a curriculum. And remember, even if your kids can't count a class as AP due to where you live or homeschool, know that this doesn't preclude them from still taking the test at the end of the school year to try to get college credit.

CLEP tests, or College-Level Examination Program tests, are a bit different. There are no high school CLEP classes. These exams are strictly for college credit. However, we found online courses that prepare students for CLEP tests. We counted the online instruction along with a purchased CLEP study guide for that subject as a high school honor's course.

What are the pros and cons of AP and CLEP tests? AP tests are only given one time at the end of the school year. CLEP tests are administered year-round at designated testing centers, so students may take the exam whenever they're ready. CLEP tests are also slightly less expensive and can be retaken in three months if your student does not get a passing score.

Note that while most universities will award AP credits depending on the score received, fewer will do so with CLEP tests – especially the more elite schools. Before committing to one of these tests, research the colleges your child hopes to attend to see what type of test credits they will accept.

To find the most up-to-date information, do an internet search with "exam credit (school name)" or "credit by exam (school name)" using the names of the universities your child is interested in attending.

Resources:
Modernstates.org – Offers free CLEP and AP classes along with reimbursement for accompanying tests. Classes are taught by college professors from top universities.

Diveintomath.com – Offers online/hybrid high school math and science classes. These classes can be modified to be regular, honors, or AP classes. In addition, CLEP/AP reviews and practice tests are also available for purchase.

Avoid bias for or against a particular subject.
I hate geometry proofs. I think they're ridiculous and a waste of time. Am I wrong? Probably. I'm also not well-read. When we started the homeschool book club at church, I had never heard of most of the books the other moms were suggesting. I can't stand poetry. It bores me to death, and I struggle to read it aloud without using a "sing-song" voice. However, my kids never knew this as they were being homeschooled. And let me tell you, it was hard to keep this to myself. I know many parents feel this way about math. From experience, I think it's best to keep these opinions to yourself and let your children decide what they like

and don't like. You may have a child that could go on to write books or be a great chemist but may not get the best education or even encouragement from a parent who's already biased against a particular subject. Try not to let your kid's opinions reflect yours. They're not you. You may be holding them back.

Do not assign every question in a textbook.
Many high school textbooks (and some middle school textbooks) have too many questions for your children to get done in a school year unless they want to do schoolwork and nothing else. In the younger grades, kids need a lot of repetition, so I do recommend full completion during those years. But in high school, for example, if your child understands the information presented in their math lesson, assign the even problems (or odd) and see how they do. Grade, review, and have them correct the ones they miss. Ensure they understand the concepts, and then move on to the next lesson. There may be some lessons that take extra time. Homeschooling is about learning the material efficiently. There is no reason to do busy work or to continue working on a concept your child has already grasped.

Sometimes syllabi are available where questions or problems have already been vetted and the best ones assigned. If you're using a textbook that doesn't include this, search online and see if you can find one. For example, *Geometry: Seeing, Doing, Understanding* by Harold R. Jacobs is an older, but excellent geometry textbook. After researching online, I found a teacher's guide from the website askdrcallahan.com. This guide included a syllabus that assigned specific problems for each section in the book. As a bonus, this website also offered video lessons for purchase and student homework help.

Stop being so busy.
In high school, my kids started to realize a few things. My son, standing 6'5" tall, would not get a basketball scholarship to the colleges he wanted to attend. After taking a year off from violin, my daughter realized that she loved having the extra time. They

both realized they liked to do things with our church youth group. And they both started to focus on their studies a bit more because we were tailoring classes to their strengths and interests.

High school is the last chance for kids to be kids. Reassess what you're spending time on and if it's worth it. If your kids are playing ball all week and then traveling for ball on the weekends, determine if that's how you want to spend your time as a family. It may or may not be. That's for you to decide. I made my son apply to one of our state's Governor's Schools - my mistake. As I mentioned earlier, he got accepted but had told me that he didn't want to go when he was initially applying. He wanted to go to church camp instead. I let him decline the invitation. He's only a kid once. He works hard during the school year and needs time to relax and have fun.

Many highly educated parents are homeschooling their kids.
My daughter's CyberPatriot team's coach is a Director of Cybersecurity with a Ph.D. His kids were homeschooled. While volunteering at our co-op one day, a mom standing next to me mentioned that her husband was an aerospace engineer that had taught at a major university and was now working for the government. I asked her if he would be willing to talk to my son, and he came to the co-op and met with us for an hour the following week. My son plays Ultimate Frisbee on a homeschool team. One Saturday morning, a dad sitting beside me was wearing a Virginia Tech hat. Since that's one of the schools my son is interested in attending, I asked him if he went there. Not only did he go there, but he's an aerospace engineer. He gave us some valuable information. The two parents running the Ultimate frisbee league are lawyers, and one is now a judge. One Saturday between games I saw the judge answering players' questions about a mock trial they were doing through their co-op. So why are all these people who have advanced degrees homeschooling their kids? There are probably many reasons, but one is that they don't trust the school systems to educate their kids properly.

Let me make something very clear. To homeschool your

children, you don't have to have a doctorate degree or be a rocket scientist. Just know that you may be sitting next to a mom or dad who is one, and you should use that to your advantage. We're all in this together, and most parents with a specific education or skill set are more than willing to share their knowledge. One homeschooling dad we've met is an electrician who talks to kids about his industry and the shortage of qualified workers. A few parents I know are artists and have been willing in the past to teach art classes and share their skills. Again, most people are more than happy to help if they can.

Not everyone needs to go to college.
Not every child is meant to go to college. Your job as a homeschool parent is to prepare them and know them well enough that you can guide them and help them realize their interests and strengths. My kids happen to be strong in STEM subjects, but your child might love to write or draw, or they might want to do something with their hands for a living. I think most of us as parents want the same thing for our children. We want them to grow up to be good people, happy, and independent as adults.

We had a young guy put a new roof on our house several years ago. It turned out that he had been homeschooled through high school and hated roofing houses. I've always wondered what steps led him into that situation. I never asked, but it made me realize that all we can do is love our kids and try to do what we think is best for them as we homeschool. If your child decides they want to go to college, it's your job to ensure they are prepared to the best of their ability. If they want to have their own business, try to arrange for them to talk with entrepreneurs. If they love working with their hands, numerous careers offer that and can be explored during the high school years. After high school, being motivated is easier if you're excited and interested in what you're working toward.

Conclusion

Our family is not unique. We don't think others need to homeschool exactly the way we have. We don't think we've done everything right along the way. I just wanted to share with those who are thinking about, have just started, or are struggling with homeschooling what has worked, what hasn't worked, and other things we've learned along the way.

I have several close friends who now homeschool. We all homeschool differently. I would never judge them for the way they do things, nor do I think they would judge me. We all love our kids and know them better than anyone else. We all do what we believe is best for our children and families. Similarly, parents who put their kids in a brick-and-mortar school shouldn't be criticized. You never truly know others' circumstances.

I recommend using this book and the suggestions as a starting point. Use what works for you. Don't be afraid to change things that aren't working along the way. Get to know other homeschooling families. Ask homeschooling parents with more experience about what has worked for them. Find out what opportunities outside the home are available in your area. These opportunities made a huge difference for us. Work within your budget. Determine what is worth spending money on and what you can do "on the cheap." And most of all, don't doubt yourself! Be consistent and keep moving forward. Your kids will reap exponential rewards in so many ways.

You can do this!

APPENDIX A

Yearly Plan Sample

Below is a sample of my daughter's seventh and my son's fifth-grade yearly plans. For most years, I did them separately. However, for this particular year I decided to combine the plans because my children were doing several subjects together. When I created this document years ago, I never expected anyone else to see it, so it may not make sense to others or be easy to understand. I'm including it here only as an example of what worked for us. This was simply a tool for me to have a written general plan for our upcoming school year and set some goals for what we hoped to achieve.

2015-2016 Yearly Plan
Katherine (K) 7th Grade
Nathan (N) 5th Grade

Math - Singapore Dimensions Math 7A&B **(K&N)**

Science - Complete Nancy Larson Science 4; Begin NL Science 5 (to be completed by end of 2016-2017 school year **(K&N)**

Spelling - Review Key cards and Phonogram cards monthly **(K&N)**

English - Rod and Staff
Grade 7 *Building Securely* **(K)**
Grade 5 *Following the Plan* **(N)**

Writing Composition/Literature
Literature and Creative Writing C @ co-op (1st semester) **(K)**
Composition 1 (2nd semester) @ co-op **(K)**
Literature and Creative Writing B @ co-op (1st semester) **(N)**
Focus on Rod and Staff English 5 (2nd semester) **(N)**
(Comp 1 @ co-op Fall 2016 **(N)**

Teaching the Classics/Monthly homeschool book club (1st and 2nd semester) **(K&N)**

Vocabulary
Vocabulary From Classical Roots Book A **(K)**
Vocabulary From Classical Roots Book 6 **(N)**

Spanish
MS Spanish I @ co-op (1st semester) **(K&N)**
MS Spanish II @ co-op (2nd semester) **(K&N)**

Music
Violin lessons/Orchestra **(K)**
Guitar lessons/ *What Your 5th Grader Needs to Know* **(N)**

Art
Misc. arts and crafts projects (1st semester) **(K&N)**
Art class @ co-op (2nd semester) **(K&N)**

PE
Volleyball (1st semester)/ TBD (2nd semester) **(K)**
Basketball(Fall/Winter)/ Flag football (Spring) **(N)**

History **(K&N)**
Veritas Press history flashcards
#17-32 New Testament, Greece, and Rome
#1-32 Middle Ages, Renaissance and Reformation
#1-32 Explorers to 1815
#1-32 1815 to present
Requirements:
1) Read each card and choose 2 sources to read from back of card.
2) Record "Title of Event" and date on next page in notebook and list the three most important facts you read about the event. You may also draw appropriate pictures as well on the page. Use one page per event. There will be no tests or worksheets.
3) Memorize all 160 cards by end of school year. Think of creative, but simple way to do this.

4) Four cards assigned per week - M,T,W,F 30-45 min/day.

(Note: August will be used to start notebook and record the previously assigned cards in the new notebook. Sources for this will not need to be re-read. - Three cards/school day in August)
(Note: 2016-2017 school year - re-read SOTW without activity book. Katherine will read 2 volumes per semester and Nathan will read 1 volume per semester.)

Geography (K&N)
1) Flashcards highlighting 50 world countries
2) World maps to complete
3) Naming all countries within a continent worksheets
4) Games - GeoDice, Rand McNalley World Facts and Landmarks flashcards, games
5) Map skills review - *What Your Third (through Sixth) Grader Needs to Know* series, geography section

(Note: Divide up work and determine weekly time allowance and productivity. 2016-2017 school year - study US geography.)

Technology
Online class (through co-op) - Intro to Scratch Programming **(K&N)**
First Lego League team (1st semester) **(K&N)**

Logic
TBD **(K)**
Chess class @ co-op (1st semester) **(N)**

Below is my daughter's 10th-grade yearly plan. As you can see, some course material was subject to change or not yet determined when I created it. However, having this in writing let me know what still needed to be planned and if her courseload looked balanced. Also, when my children started high school, I began including how many credits they would recieve for each class to help me ensure they were staying on track to graduate.

2018-2019 Yearly Plan
Katherine 10th Grade

Elective - 1/2 Credit
Drivers Ed - Drive For Life Academy

Bible - 1/4 Credit
Books of Poetry/ Major Prophets (1st semester)
Minor Prophets/ Gospels w/ focus on Mark (2nd semester)
@ home w/ KCS CD

English - 1 Credit
1) Composition/Literature B (2-hr course) @ co-op
2) *Vocbulary From Classical Roots* Book D @ home
3) Mom's Reading List:
  1. *The Great Gatsby*
  2. *I Have a Dream and Letter From Birmingham Jail*
  3. *How Should We Then Live?*
  4. *Animal Farm*
  5. *John Adams*

Math - 1 Credit
Algebra and Trigonometry by Foerster @ home

Science - 1 Credit
Chemistry (2-hr course) @ co-op
Textbook assigned by co-op instructor

History - 1 Credit
The Great Courses video series (TBD) @ home

Foreign Language - 1 Credit
Spanish II (co-op/online class)

Elective - 1 Credit
Critical Thinking @ co-op

Personal Finance - 1/2 Credit
Dave Ramsey - *Foundations* @ home

ACT Prep
Prep Book - TBD

APPENDIX B
Weekly Schedule Sample

The following spreadsheet is a page from one of my teacher's planners. It shows a sample schedule for the first semester of my daughter's seventh and my son's fifth-grade school years. I would create a schedule at the beginning of each semester and use it as a template. It was only a guide and was subject to change for any given week, day, or hour.

A written weekly schedule allowed me to see the most efficient way to plan our days. If this were an actual week, I would have had lessons or page numbers assigned to each subject. I've only included this as an example of what worked for us. If you know of a better system, then definitely use that. The primary purpose of weekly planning is to keep your homeschooling on track. Do it the way it works best for you and your family.

Week of			KATHERINE	NATHAN		
Time	**Monday**	**Time**	**Tuesday**	**Time**	**Wednesday**	
9:00-	Math	9:00-	Math	9:00-	Math	
9:00-	Math	9:00-	Math	9:00-	Math	
10:00	Science	10:00	Grammar	10:00	Science	
10:00	Science	10_00	Grammar	10:00	Science	
11:00-	Grammar	11:00-	Vocabulary	11:00-	Grammar	
11:00-	Grammar	11:00-	Vocabulary	11:00-	Grammar	
12:00	Lunch	11:30-	Geography	12:00	Histiry	
12:00	Lunch	11:30-	Geography	12:00	History	
12:30	History/Geography	12:00	Lunch	12:30	Lunch	
12:30	History/Geography	12:00	Lunch	12:30	Lunch	
1:30-	Logic/Instument Practice	1:00-	Violin Lessons	12:30	Independent study/reading/instrumen	
1:30-	Logic/Instrument Practice	1:00-	Independent Study/Reading/Instrume	12:30	Independent study/reading/instrumen	
6:30-	Orchestra Rehearsal - K		Lego League Practice - K&N	3:00-	Guitar Lessons - N	
	(Possible Bball or Vball practice)		(Possible Bball or Vball practice)	4:00-	Church Homeschool Event/Fieldtrip -	
	DINNER		DINNER		DINNER	

Time	**Thursday**	**Time**	**Friday**	**Saturday**	**Sunday**
9::00-	Spanish Class	9:00-	Math		
9:00-	Spanish Class	9:00-	Math		
10:00	Study Hall	10:00	English Composition/Complete Co-		
10:00	Study Hall	10:00	English Composition/Complete Co-		
11:00-	English Composition Class	11:00-	Grammar		
11:00-	Chess Class	11:00-	Grammar		
12:00	Lunch	12:30	Lunch		
12:00	Lunoh	12:30	Lunch		
1:00-	History Fun Class	1:00-	History		
1:00-	History Fun Class	1:00-	History		
2:00-	Stock Market Cass	2:00-	Book Club (monthly) or Literature Re		
2:00-	English Composition Class	2:00-	Book Club (monthly) or Literature Re		
			Lego League Practice		
	(Possible Bball or Vball practice)				
	DINNER		DINNER		

APPENDIX C
Our Favorite Curriculums

Singapore Math

We used *Singapore Primary Mathematics Standards Edition* math curriculum from kindergarten through sixth grade. Then, we used *Singapore Dimensions Math* for the seventh and eighth grades. There are newer versions available now and video instruction also. Unfortunately, this curriculum ends at the eighth-grade level. However, it gave both of my kids a strong foundation in math which helped them do well in their high school and dual enrollment math classes.

My son loved it! My daughter did not, and some days were excruciating trying to get her to focus long enough to get a lesson done. She may not have realized it then, but this curriculum eventually helped her become a solid math student. My husband and I laugh at the irony that she'll graduate from college in a few years with a math minor and is happy about it!

The things I loved the most about this curriculum were the colorful pages and illustrations. They made a subject that can be intimidating or boring seem more relatable.

All About Spelling

As I mentioned previously, this curriculum helped my daughter learn to spell when a workbook approach wasn't working. I loved this spelling program! It took some preparation at the beginning to figure out how I would teach it, but we never looked back once we started. *All About Spelling* uses a multisensory approach to teaching through sight, sound, and touch. It was developed by a mother who was told her nine-year-old son had such severe dyslexia that he would never be able to read or spell.

This program was thorough and answered all our questions about why a word is spelled and pronounced the way it is. There are seven levels based on mastery of the material rather than grade level. I can confidently say this curriculum left no gaps in my children's spelling education. It is solid! It's also easy to do with multiple-aged children if they are just a few years apart.

All About Reading is also available. I didn't use it to teach either of my children to read. I'm not sure if it wasn't available yet or if I just hadn't heard about it. If I were to teach reading to a child again, I would use this curriculum in a heartbeat! There are in-depth reviews on cathyduffyreviews.com for *All About Spelling* and *All About Reading*. Both are definitely worth researching and considering for your homeschool.

First Language Lessons – Level 1
We used all four levels of this language arts curriculum starting in first grade. Level 1 was my favorite. It was such a sweet, soft introduction to learning for a young child. The lessons were simple and fun and we looked forward to doing them.

When we finished the *First Language Lessons* series, we moved on to Rod and Staff English. This was a serious "meat and potatoes" curriculum. It was a lot of work, and my kids were not big fans. There was so much to cover that we did most of the lessons orally, and then I would assign a few sentences to diagram. Some will think Rod and Staff English is a little dated in the subject matter of the practice exercises and in the way it emphasizes diagramming sentences. But I liked it. And my kids know their grammar, that's for sure!

Nancy Larson® Science
I was so thankful to find this science curriculum. It's scripted for the instructor and can be done with multiple children simultaneously. In fact, I think my children doing it together made it more fun for all of us. I had tried several ways to teach

science in elementary school, but nothing seemed to work well. I wanted fun, relevant experiments and a teacher's guide to help me answer all my children's "why" questions. Nancy Larson® Science gave that to me. It was this curriculum that initially piqued my children's interests in different areas of science.

I almost ruled this curriculum out because it's written from a secular perspective. However, I am glad I didn't because it allowed me to present a different view from what was taught in the few lessons where this was an issue. My children learned what my perspective was and why their dad and I hold different beliefs from the author. They also learned that people have differing opinions and that just because something is spoken or written doesn't necessarily make it true. My children began to learn how to think critically around this time, and Nancy Larson® Science started that process.

Similarly, don't immediately rule out a faith-based curriculum if you come from a secular background. Many of these are academically solid and well-written. Using them may present discussion opportunities on deeper topics as your children age. These conversations, however, require the parent to know what they believe and why they believe it and to be able to communicate that to their child.

The Story of the World

We went through this history curriculum twice. Four books cover ancient through modern times, and each volume is designed to be completed in a school year. The first time we went through it, we used the accompanying activity book, which provided maps, coloring pages, art activities, reading suggestions, and more. The reading suggestions were for all ages, so the second time my kids went through the books, we did fewer crafts and chose more in-depth reading selections. There are also test booklets available for purchase.

Each lesson is in narrative form, which helped keep my children's interest when they were younger. Sometimes I would let them draw or quietly play while I read. The second time they went through the four books, they read them independently.

This was the first time I had heard the history of the Bible put into a timeline with other world histories. It was more fascinating to me than to my children. I had never realized before teaching *The Story of the World* that I hadn't learned history chronologically in school. Learning it this way is enlightening and meaningful. I highly recommend it!

Vocabulary From Classical Roots

I loved this supplemental curriculum. It teaches Greek and Latin roots to help students expand their English vocabulary. The publisher suggests the workbooks be used from fourth through twelfth grade. There are twenty lessons, including reviews, in each workbook. We did one workbook per year, and I would assign a lesson to be completed every two weeks. The work was done independently, and then we would grade it together.

While I decided early on that we would not spend our time learning Latin; I do think knowing Greek and Latin roots is beneficial. I realize these workbooks are "one more thing to do," but they are worth it. This was time well spent for my kids. The English language started to make more sense to them as they worked through this curriculum, and what they've learned continues to help them make educated guesses on the meanings of difficult words.

ABOUT THE AUTHOR

Beth Spann

Beth Spann, a homeschool mom and optometrist, lives in Tennessee with her husband and teenage son while her daughter is away at college. Wistful that her homeschooling days are almost behind her, she is ready to embrace the next chapter of her life.

Made in United States
Orlando, FL
01 February 2023